10 Minute Guide to Quattro Pro® 4

Revised by Joe Kraynak

A Division of Prentice Hall Computer Publishing
11711 North College, Carmel, Indiana 46032 USA

© **1992 by Sams**

All rights reserved. No part of this book shall be reproduced, stored in a retrieval system, or transmitted by any means, electronic, mechanical, photocopying, recording, or otherwise, without written permission from the publisher. No patent liability is assumed with respect to the use of the information contained herein. While every precaution has been taken in the preparation of this book, the publisher and authors assume no responsibility for errors or omissions. Neither is any liability assumed for damages resulting from the use of the information contained herein. For more information, write to Sams, 11711 North College Avenue, Suite 141, Carmel, Indiana 46032.

International Standard Book Number: 0-672-30255-1
Library of Congress Catalog Card Number: 91-68209

95 94 93 92   8 7 6 5 4 3 2 1

Interpretation of the printing code: the rightmost double-digit number is the year of the book's printing; the rightmost single-digit number is the number of the book's printing. For example, a printing code of 92-1 shows that the first printing of the book was in 1992.

Publisher: *Richard K. Swadley*
Associate Publisher: *Marie Butler-Knight*
Managing Editor: *Elizabeth Keaffaber*
Development Editor: *Faithe Wempen*
Copy Editor: *Ronda Carter Henry*
Designer: *Michele Laseau*
Cover Design: *Dan Armstrong*
Indexer: *Tina Trettin*
Production: *Claudia Bell, Mike Britton, Brad Chinn, Joelynn Gifford, Dennis Clay Hager, Debbie Hanna, Bob LaRoche, Laurie Lee, David McKenna, Matthew Morrill, Anne Owen, Dennis Sheehan, Ann Taylor, Corinne Walls, Mary Beth Wakefield, Jenny Watson*

Special thanks to C. Herbert Feltner for ensuring the technical accuracy of this book.

Screen reproductions in this book were created by means of the program Collage Plus from Inner Media, Inc., Hollis, NH.

Printed in the United States of America

Contents

Introduction, ix

1 Starting and Exiting Quattro Pro, 1

Starting Quattro Pro, 1
Changing the Screen Mode, 2
Getting Help, 5
Exiting Quattro Pro, 7

2 Moving Around the Worksheet, 9

The Worksheet Screen, 9
Moving the Selector with the Keyboard, 11
Moving the Selector with the Mouse, 13

3 Entering Commands in Quattro Pro, 16

Quattro Pro Menus, 16
Responding to Dialog Boxes, 19
Quick Command Access with the SpeedBar, 21

4 Entering Labels and Values, 24

Understanding Worksheet Data, 24
Entering Labels, 25
Entering Values, 28
Entering Dates, 29

5 Entering Formulas, 31

Understanding Formulas, 31
Order of Operations, 33
Entering Formulas, 34
Using Absolute Cell References, 35
Changing the Recalculation Setting, 37

6 Entering Functions, 39

Understanding Functions, 39
Entering Functions, 39
Using TurboSum, 41
Logical Operators, 43

7 Saving, Closing, and Opening Worksheets, 45

Saving Worksheets, 45
Closing a Worksheet File, 48
Opening or Retrieving a Worksheet, 49
Switching Windows, 50

8 Selecting Cell Blocks, 51

Cells and Cell Blocks, 51
Selecting a Cell Block, 51
Specifying a Range of Cells, 53

9 Naming Cells and Ranges, 56

Using Named Cells and Ranges, 56
Naming a Cell, 57
Naming a Range, 58
Finding Cells by Their Names, 58
Making a Table of Cell Names, 59

10 Editing Cells, 60

Editing the Contents of a Cell, 60
Deleting Cell Contents, 62
Insert and Overstrike, 62
Copying the Contents and Formatting of Cells, 62
Moving a Cell Block, 64
Undoing Changes, 65

11 Controlling Columns and Rows, 66

Changing Column Width, 66
Changing Row Height, 69
Inserting a Row or Column, 70
Deleting Rows or Columns, 72

12 Enhancing the Appearance of Labels and Values, 73

Formatting Values, 73
Changing Fonts, 75
Aligning Text in Cells, 78
Protecting Cell Contents, 79

13 Adding Lines and Shading to Cells and Blocks, 80

Drawing Lines Around and Between Cells, 80
Shading a Cell or Cell Block, 81

14 Formatting Cells with Styles, 84

Understanding Styles, 84
Applying Existing Styles, 85
Creating Custom Styles, 86
Changing Styles, 87

15 Setting Up a Page for Printing, 89

Setting Up a Page, 89
Adding a Header and Footer, 90
Setting the Page Length and Margins, 92
Selecting a Paper Orientation, 93
Automatic Page Breaks, 94
Scaling the Printout, 95
Updating the Print Settings, 95

16 Printing a Worksheet, 96

Selecting a Printer, 96
Selecting Print Options, 97
Seeing Your Worksheet in Print Preview Mode, 99
Printing a Hard Copy of Your Worksheet, 102

17 Creating Graphs, 103

Quattro Pro Graphs, 103
Selecting the Cells To Graph, 104
Viewing Your Graph, 106
Adding Graph Titles and Legends, 107
Saving, Retrieving, and Inserting Graphs, 109

18 Enhancing and Printing Graphs, 112

Enhancing Your Graph, 112
Annotating Your Graph, 116
Printing a Graph, 119

19 Creating a Simple Database, 120

Database Basics, 120
Creating a Database, 122
Saving the Database, 123

20 Sorting, Searching, and Printing a Database, 124

Sorting a Database, 124
Modifying the Sort Rules, 126
Searching for Records, 127
Extracting Records, 131
Printing a Database Report, 132

21 Managing Your Files, 133

Running the File Manager, 133
Making a Directory, 136
Selecting Files, 136
Copying and Moving Files, 137
Erasing Files, 138
Renaming Files, 138

A Table of Functions, 139

Mathematical Functions, 139
Statistical Functions, 139
String Functions, 140
Financial Functions, 140
Date and Time Functions, 141
Database Statistical Functions, 142

B *Table of Features, 144*

C *DOS Primer, 146*
   Starting DOS, 146
   Working with Disks, 147
   Changing to a Directory, 151
   Is That All?, 152

   Index, 153

Introduction

Perhaps you walked into work this morning and found Quattro Pro 4 on your desk. A note is stuck to the box: "We need a budget for the upcoming meeting. See what you can do."

Now What?

You could wade through the manual that came with the program to find out how to perform a specific task, but that may take a while and it may tell you more than you want to know. You need a practical guide, one that will tell you exactly how to create and print a spreadsheet and graph for the meeting.

Welcome to the *10 Minute Guide to Quattro Pro 4*

Because most people don't have the luxury of sitting down uninterrupted for hours at a time to learn Quattro Pro, this *10 Minute Guide* does not attempt to teach *everything* about the program. Instead, it focuses on the most often-used features. Each feature is covered in a single self-contained lesson, which is designed to take 10 minutes or less to complete.

The *10 Minute Guide* teaches you about the program without relying on technical jargon. With straightforward, easy-to-follow explanations and numbered lists that tell you what keys to press and what options to select, the *10 Minute Guide to Quattro Pro 4* makes learning the program quick and easy.

Who Should Use the *10 Minute Guide to Quattro Pro 4?*

The *10 Minute Guide to Quattro Pro 4* is for anyone who

- Needs to learn Quattro Pro quickly.
- Feels overwhelmed or intimidated by the complexity of the Quattro Pro program.
- Wants to find out quickly whether Quattro Pro will meet his or her computing needs.
- Wants a clear, concise guide to the most important features of Quattro Pro.

What Is Quattro Pro?

Quattro Pro is an advanced spreadsheet program. Using a familiar row-and-column format, Quattro Pro allows you to manipulate data in a variety of ways. Instead of using ledger paper, a calculator, and a pencil, you can use Quattro Pro to do both simple and complex number-crunching activities.

Introduction

How To Use This Book

The *10 Minute Guide to Quattro Pro 4* consists of a series of lessons ranging from basic startup to a few more advanced features. If this is your first encounter with Quattro Pro, you should probably work through Lessons 1 to 11 in order. These lessons lead you through the process of creating, editing, and printing a spreadsheet. Subsequent lessons tell you how to use the more advanced features to customize your spreadsheet, use your spreadsheet as a database, and create, enhance, and print graphs.

If Quattro Pro has not been installed on your computer, consult the DOS Primer at the end of this book to learn how to make backup copies of your Quattro Pro program disks and then look to the inside front cover for installation steps.

Icons and Conventions Used in This Book

The following icons have been used throughout the book to help you find your way around:

Timesaver Tip icons offer shortcuts and hints for using the program efficiently.

Plain English icons define new terms.

Panic Button icons appear where new users often run into trouble.

xi

The following conventions have been used to clarify the steps you must perform:

`On-screen text`. Any text that appears on-screen is shown in a special type called monospace.

What you `type`. The information you type appears in second color monospace.

Menu Names. The names of menus, commands, buttons, and dialog boxes are shown with the first letter capitalized for easy recognition.

Option selections. In Quattro Pro, you can select an option by using your mouse or by typing the highlighted selection letter in the option's name. In this book, any item you need to select, choose, use, and so forth is shown in color. The highlighted selection letter that corresponds to the highlighted letter you see on-screen is in bold as well.

Trademarks

All terms mentioned in this book that are known to be trademarks or service marks are listed below. In addition, terms suspected of being trademarks or service marks have been appropriately capitalized. Sams cannot attest to the accuracy of this information. Use of a term in this book should not be regarded as affecting the validity of any trademark or service mark.

Quattro Pro 4 is a registered trademark or Borland International, Inc.

MS-DOS is a registered trademark of Microsoft Corporation.

Lotus and 1-2-3 are registered trademarks of Lotus Development Corporation.

Lessons

Lesson 1
Starting and Exiting Quattro Pro

In this lesson, you'll learn how to start and end a typical Quattro Pro work session and how to use Quattro Pro's Help feature.

Starting Quattro Pro

Before you can run Quattro Pro, it must be installed on your computer's hard disk. If you have not installed Quattro Pro, refer to the inside front cover of this book for instructions. Once Quattro Pro is installed, follow these steps to run it:

1. Change to the drive that contains the Quattro Pro directory (for example, type `c:` and press Enter).

2. Change to the directory that contains your Quattro Pro program files (for example, type `cd\qpro` and press Enter).

3. Type `q` and press Enter.

The Quattro Pro opening screen appears, and then the worksheet screen, shown in Figure 1.1, appears.

1

Lesson 1

If you have a mouse installed on your computer, Quattro Pro automatically detects the mouse type and activates the mouse pointer, shown in Figure 1.1. Quattro Pro's *SpeedBar* also appears if a mouse is detected. The SpeedBar provides a quick way to select common commands with the mouse; you'll learn more about it in Lesson 3.

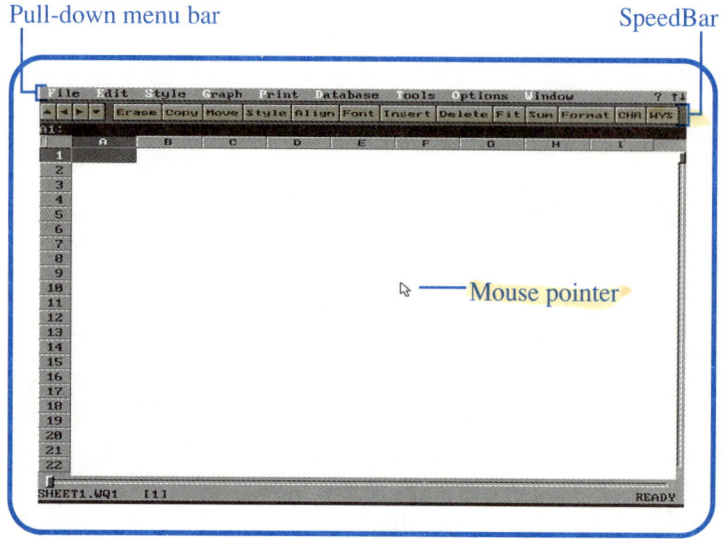

Figure 1.1 The Quattro Pro worksheet screen.

Changing the Screen Mode

When you installed Quattro Pro 4, you chose whether to display the screen in *WYSIWYG* or character mode. If you chose character mode (so Quattro Pro would run faster), you may want to switch to WYSIWYG mode to view your spreadsheet as it will appear in print.

Starting and Exiting Quattro Pro

Graphics Display Card Needed To switch to WYSIWYG mode a graphics display card must be installed in your system.

WYSIWYG WYSIWYG is the acronym for **What You See Is What You Get.** WYSIWYG mode enables you to display your work on-screen as it will look when it is printed. All screenshots in this book are captured in WYSIWYG mode unless specifically noted otherwise.

To change the screen display mode, follow these steps:

1. Press / (the forward slash) to activate the *pull-down menu* and then press **o**. Or click on Options in the menu bar (if you are unfamiliar with mouse terminology or how to use the mouse, refer to Lesson 2). The , shown in Figure 1.2, appears.

2. Select the Display Mode option by pressing **D** or by clicking on Display Mode. Quattro Pro displays a list of possible screen modes.

3. Highlight the mode you want and press Enter, or press the letter that corresponds to the desired display mode (**A** is usually character mode, and **B** is WYSIWYG).

Quattro Pro returns to the worksheet screen in the new display mode. A sample screen in character mode is shown in Figure 1.3. The Mouse Palette on the right corresponds to the SpeedBar in WYSIWYG mode.

3

Lesson 1

Choosing Other Modes The other modes on this menu allow you to choose a specific display adapter. Do not choose any of these options unless you are sure your computer is properly equipped.

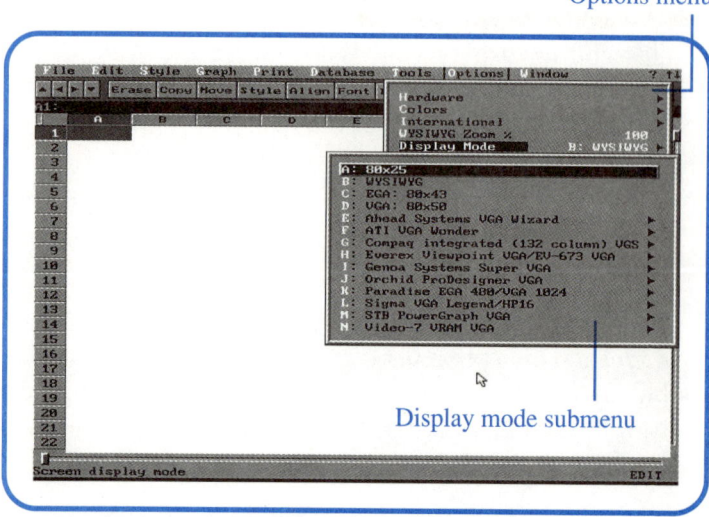

Figure 1.2 The Options pull-down menu with the Display Mode submenu.

Pull-down Menu In the preceding steps, the term *pull-down menu* was used. For more information on how to use pull-down menus, refer to Lesson 3.

Switching Modes with the SpeedBar A quicker way to switch from WYSIWYG mode to character mode is to use the SpeedBar. Click on the CHR button to change to character mode. Once you are in character mode, you must use the /Options Display Mode submenu to return to WYSIWYG mode.

4

Starting and Exiting Quattro Pro

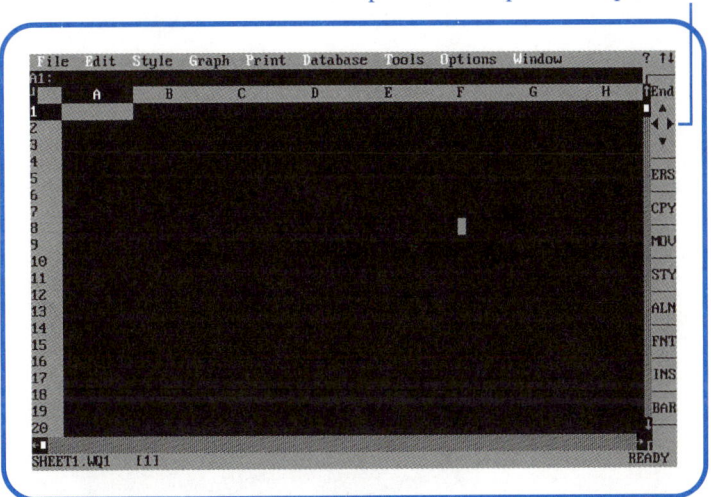

Figure 1.3 A blank worksheet screen displayed in character mode.

Getting Help

Quattro Pro's Help feature is *context-sensitive,* which means that at any time you can get help for the task you are currently trying to perform. For example, if you are building a graph and you select Help, Quattro Pro will display a Graph help screen. In Figure 1.4, the Help screen has been accessed from a blank worksheet. The following steps explain how to use the Help feature:

1. Press F1 or click on ? in the menu bar. The Quattro Pro Help Topics screen appears, as shown in Figure 1.4. A list of help topics is displayed, followed by a brief description of each topic.

5

Lesson 1

2. Highlight a topic and press Enter, or click on a topic to view a Help screen with information about that topic. Another Help screen appears, offering more specific information about the selected topic.

3. Press Esc to close the Help screen.

Select a topic to view more information.

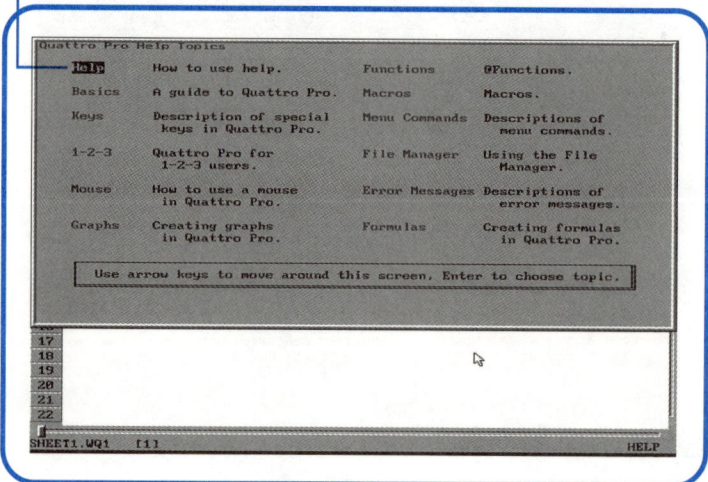

Figure 1.4 The Quattro Pro Help Topics screen.

Quick Access to a Help Topic To find information about a specific help topic, press F1 and then press F3. The Help Index appears, as shown in Figure 1.5. Start typing the name of the topic for which you want help. As you type, the cursor moves to a help topic in the list that matches the characters you typed.

Starting and Exiting Quattro Pro

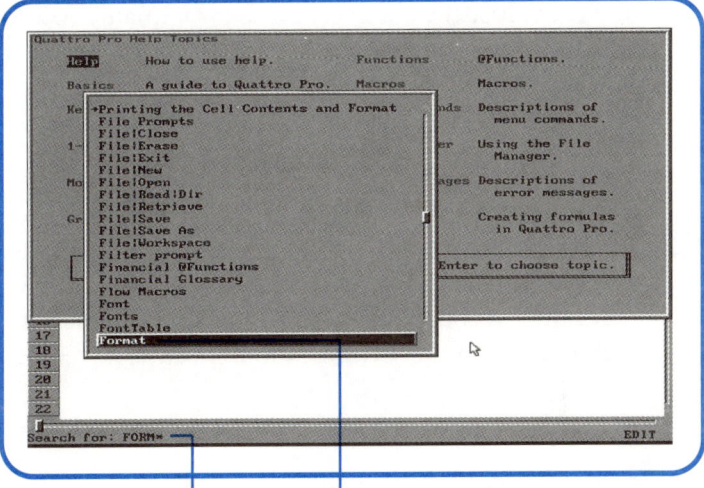

The text you type appears here.

The cursor jumps to the first topic that matches the characters you type.

Figure 1.5 Use the Help Index to find information quickly.

Exiting Quattro Pro

To exit Quattro Pro and return to DOS after finishing a work session, follow these steps:

1. Press / (forward slash) to activate the menu bar, and then press F. Or click on File in the menu bar. This opens the File menu.

2. Press x to select Exit with the keyboard, or click on Exit with the mouse.

3. If you made changes to the worksheet without saving them, Quattro Pro displays a *dialog box* asking you if

7

Lesson 1

you want to lose the changes. Lesson 7 explains how to name and save a worksheet.

4. If the dialog box appears, select Yes to exit.

Exiting Quickly   The speed key combination for exiting Quattro Pro is Ctrl-X (hold down the Ctrl key and press X). If you haven't saved your changes, a dialog box appears, asking if you want to lose your changes. To find out more about *speed keys,* refer to Lesson 3.

Dialog Box   A dialog box is a box that appears on-screen that conveys or requests more information to perform an operation. For more information about responding to dialog boxes, see Lesson 3.

In this lesson, you learned how to start and exit Quattro Pro, change the screen display mode, and get help. In the next lesson, you will learn how to navigate the Quattro Pro worksheet.

Lesson 2
Moving Around the Worksheet

In this lesson, you'll learn how to move quickly around the worksheet using the keyboard and the mouse.

The Worksheet Screen

A worksheet is divided into *cells*. Cells are created by the intersection of numbered *rows* and alphabetized *columns* (rows run left to right; columns run up and down). If you are in WYSIWYG mode, you can see the gridlines that outline the cells. If they're not visible, open the Window menu and choose Options, Grid Lines, and then Display. Figure 2.1 shows the screen in WYSIWYG mode with the gridlines displayed.

The following list explains the parts of the worksheet screen:

Menu Bar: The bar across the top of the screen contains the names of pull-down menus. Each pull-down menu contains a series of commands.

9

Lesson 2

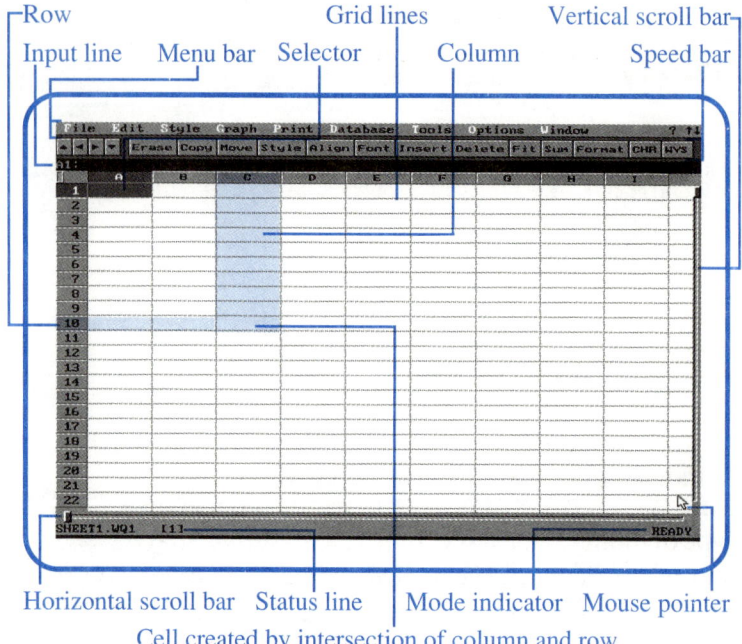

Figure 2.1 The Quattro Pro worksheet screen (shown in WYSIWYG mode with gridlines displayed).

Input Line: This line displays the location of the *selector*. When you enter data in a cell, it first appears on the input line. When you press Enter, the data on the input line is inserted in the cell.

Selector: The selector is a rectangular highlight that appears in the active cell. When a worksheet is first opened, the selector is in cell A1.

Mouse Pointer: In WYSIWYG mode, the mouse pointer resembles an arrowhead; in character mode, it is a small rectangle.

Status Line: This line displays the name of the worksheet, or when a menu is pulled down, a description of the highlighted option.

Mode Indicator: The mode indicator (on the status line) indicates the operating state Quattro Pro is in. Usually, Quattro Pro is waiting for cell input so the mode indicator reads READY.

Moving the Selector with the Keyboard

The appearance of the selector varies, depending on the type of monitor you have. If, for example, you have a black-and-white monitor, the selector appears in reverse video; the selector itself is black, and any text it highlights is white. On a color monitor, it appears in a different color. When you open a new worksheet, the selector is in cell A1. Table 2.1 explains the keystrokes you use to move the selector in Quattro Pro.

Table 2.1 Selector movement keys.

Press	To move
→	Right one cell
←	Left one cell
↓	Down one cell
↑	Up one cell
Tab	Right one screen
Shift-Tab	Left one screen
Home	Cell A1

continues

Lesson 2

Table 2.1   continued

Press	To move
PgDn	Down one screen
PgUp	Up one screen
End-↑, ↓, ←, or →	In the direction of the arrow to the first cell that contains data or to the first or last cell in the row or column

Place the selector in cell A1 and try the following steps to get a feel for moving the selector with the keyboard:

1. Press ↓. The selector should now be located in cell A2, and the input line displays A2.

2. Press ↑ twice. The first time you press the key, the selector moves to cell A1. After that, Quattro Pro beeps to let you know that you have reached the top of the worksheet.

3. Press PgDn. The selector jumps down a full screen.

4. Press Home. The selector jumps back to cell A1.

5. Press Tab. The selector jumps a full screen to the right.

6. Press Home to move the selector back to cell A1.

7. Press End and then press ↓. The selector immediately jumps to the bottom row of the worksheet, row 8192.

8. Press End and then press →. The selector jumps to the cell farthest to the right of cell A1, cell IV8192.

9. Press Home. The selector returns to cell A1.

—*Moving Around the Worksheet*

The portion of the worksheet you see on-screen at once is small compared to the total number of cells—2,097,152! Each worksheet has 256 columns by 8,192 rows. Figure 2.2 gives you a perspective of the screen versus the entire worksheet.

Screen

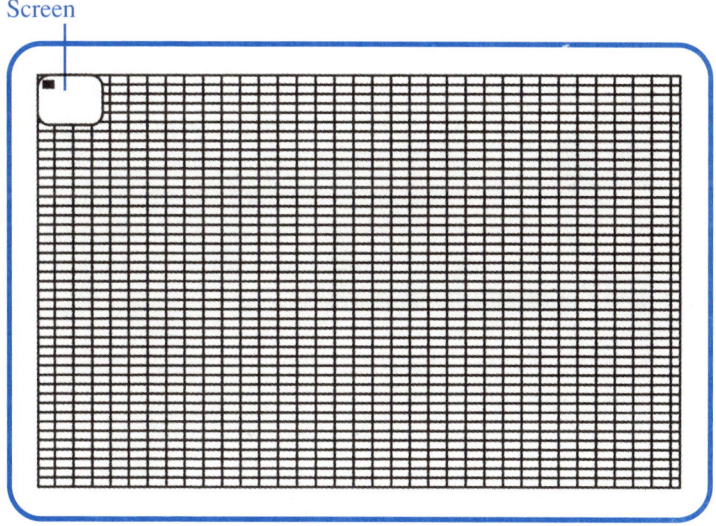

Figure 2.2 The screen in proportion to the total amount of space in the worksheet.

Moving the Selector with the Mouse

If you have not used a mouse before, familiarize yourself with the following terms used to describe mouse movements:

Point   Move the tip of the mouse pointer onto an item on the screen or into a cell.

13

Lesson 2

Click   Press and release the mouse button once, without moving the mouse. If your mouse has more than one button, press the left button (unless specifically instructed to use the right button).

Drag   Hold down the left mouse button while moving the mouse pointer.

If you are using the mouse, you can use the buttons on the left end of the SpeedBar to move the selector in the worksheet (see Figure 2.3). Clicking on one of these buttons is equivalent to pressing the End key and then pressing an arrow key. It moves the selector in the direction of the arrow to the first cell that contains data or to the first or last cell in the current row or column.

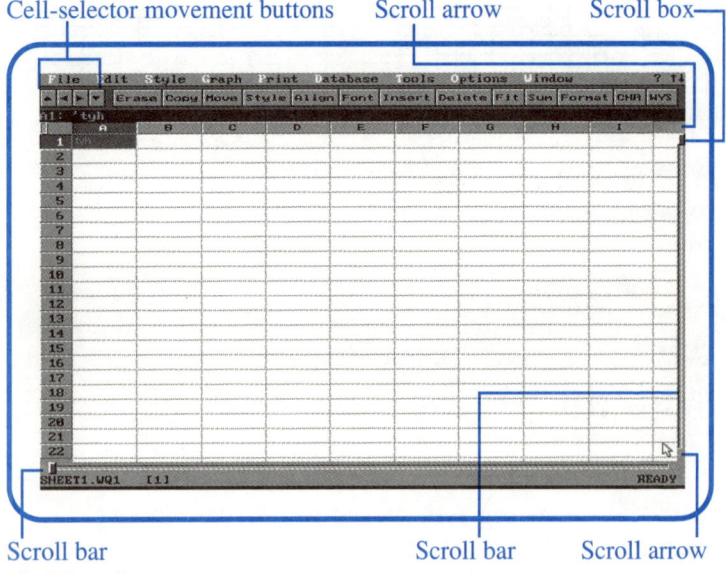

Figure 2.3   The SpeedBar.

Moving Around the Worksheet

If the portion of the worksheet you want to move to is off the screen, you can bring it into view using the scroll bars (see Figure 2.3):

Scroll Arrows: Click on the arrows at either end of the scroll bar to move incrementally in the direction of the arrow.

Scroll Box: Drag the scroll box along the scroll bar to the area of the worksheet you want to view. For example, to move to the middle of the spreadsheet, drag the scroll box to the middle of the scroll bar.

Scroll Bar: Click once inside the scroll bar on either side of the scroll box to move the view one screenful at a time.

Left-Handed Mouse To set up the mouse for left-handed use, open the Options menu and select Hardware, Mouse Button, and Right (to make the right mouse button active). Select Update from the Options menu to save your changes for the next work session and then choose Quit. Now, whenever you are told to click the mouse button, click the right mouse button instead, and vice versa.

In this lesson, you learned how to move around the worksheet screen with the mouse and the keyboard. In the next lesson, you will learn how to enter various commands in Quattro Pro.

15

Lesson 3

Entering Commands in Quattro Pro

In this lesson, you'll learn how to enter commands using the pull-down menus, the SpeedBar, and Quattro Pro's shortcut keys, and how to respond to dialog boxes.

Quattro Pro Menus

At the top of the worksheet screen is the menu bar containing the names of the pull-down menus. In Lesson 1, you opened the **O**ptions pull-down menu to change the screen display mode, and you opened the **F**ile menu to exit Quattro Pro. Figure 3.1 shows the File menu pulled down.

Pull-Down Menus The term *pull-down menu* refers to a menu that remains hidden in the menu bar until you press a key combination or use the mouse to open or pull down the menu. This keeps the menus from taking up space on-screen until you need them.

Entering Commands in Quattro Pro

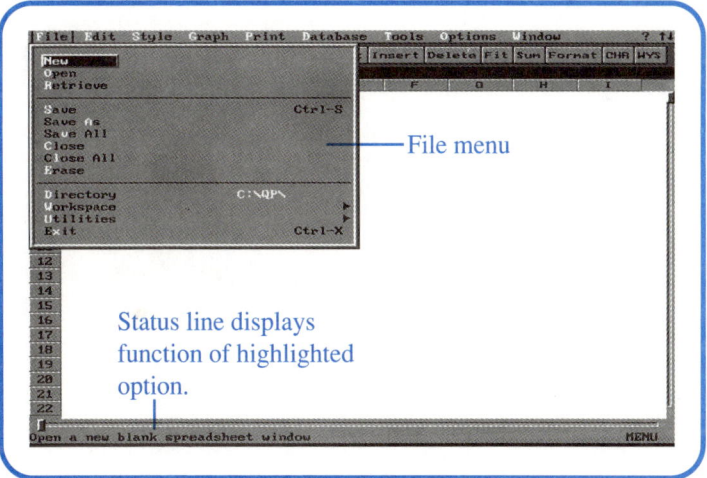

Figure 3.1 The File menu pulled down.

Using the Mouse To Select Options

To select an option from a pull-down menu using your mouse, take the following steps:

1. Move the mouse pointer over the desired menu name and click the left mouse button.

2. Click on the desired option in the menu. If the option is followed by a right-pointing arrow, a submenu or dialog box appears (see Figure 3.2).

3. If a submenu appears, click on the desired option. If a dialog box appears, enter the required information as explained later in this lesson.

4. To close the menu without entering a command, click anywhere outside the menu or dialog box.

17

Lesson 3

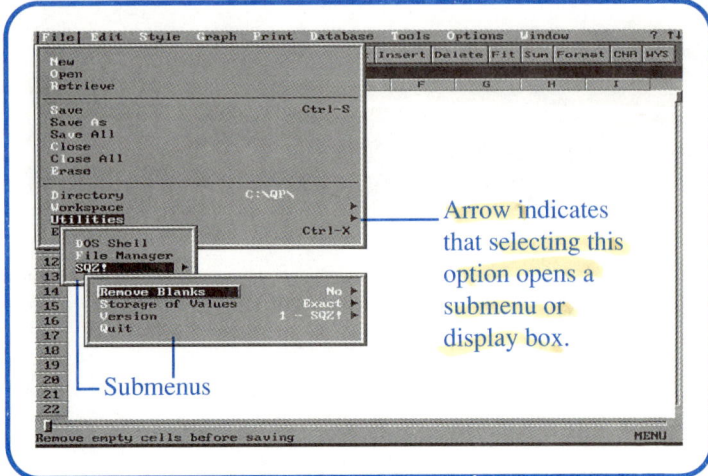

Figure 3.2 Selecting an option that is followed by an arrow opens a submenu or dialog box.

Using the Keyboard To Select Options

To select an option from a pull-down menu using your keyboard, take the following steps:

1. Press / and then press the highlighted letter in the menu's name. For example, to open the File menu, press / and then F.

2. Use the arrow keys to highlight the desired option and then press Enter. Or type the highlighted letter in the option's name.

3. If a submenu appears, highlight the desired option on the submenu and press Enter. Or type the highlighted letter in the option's name. If a dialog box appears, enter the required information as explained later in this lesson.

18

Entering Commands in Quattro Pro

4. To close the menu or dialog box without selecting an option, press the Esc key.

Switching Menus Once a menu is pulled down, you can switch to a different menu by pressing ← or →. The current menu is then closed, and the menu to the left or right is opened.

Using Ctrl-Key Shortcuts

Several menu options have corresponding *shortcut keys;* for example, to the right of **S**ave on the **F**ile menu is the shortcut key Ctrl-S. These shortcut keys allow you to bypass the pull-down menus. Instead of opening the **F**ile menu and choosing **S**ave, you can press Ctrl-S to enter the **S**ave command.

Responding to Dialog Boxes

Many options on the pull-down menus display a dialog box when selected. For example, if you select the **L**ayout command from the **P**rint menu, you'll see the Print Layout Options dialog box, as shown in Figure 3.3. Dialog boxes contain one or more of the following elements:

Option Buttons: You can select only one option button in a group of option buttons. These buttons are commonly called *radio buttons* because when you press one button it deactivates the other button, as in a car radio.

Text Entries: Some options require you to type an entry. For example, to change the page length, you must type an entry to specify the number of lines long you want the page to be.

19

Lesson 3

Command Buttons: All dialog boxes contain at least one command button that lets you close the dialog box. Most dialog boxes contain at least two command buttons: one for executing the command and one for canceling it.

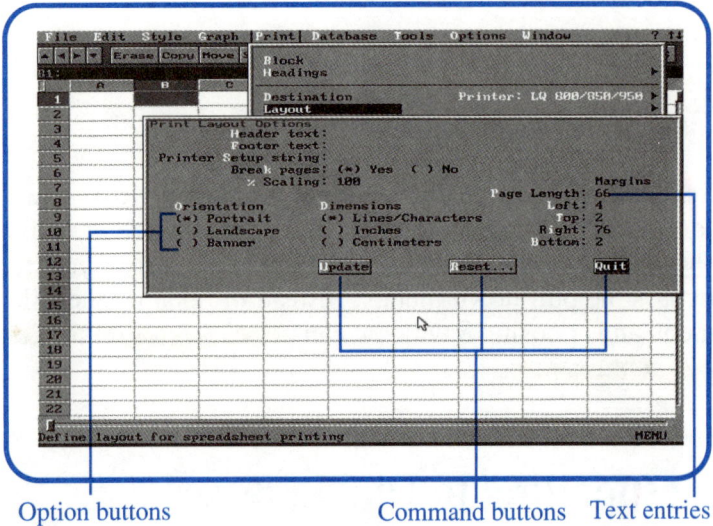

Option buttons   Command buttons   Text entries

Figure 3.3 With any dialog box, you select the desired options and then press a command button to execute the commands.

Responding to Dialog Boxes Using the Mouse

To move around in a dialog box with the mouse, click on the desired option, selection, or button. For example, to change the Break Pages setting from **Yes** to **No**, click on **Yes**. If the selected option requires you to type a setting, type the setting. Click on one of the command buttons to put your changes into effect.

Entering Commands in Quattro Pro

Responding to Dialog Boxes Using the Keyboard

Using a keyboard to get around in a dialog box is a little trickier. You should first note that every dialog box contains several options. To move from one option to another, press Tab. To move back one option, press Shift-Tab. You can also move from one option to another by pressing the key that corresponds to the highlighted letter in the option's name.

Once you select an option, you can select setting(s) for the option by pressing the ↑ or ↓ key to highlight the setting and then pressing Enter. You can also choose a setting by pressing the key that corresponds to the highlighted letter in the setting's name.

Quick Command Access with the SpeedBar

Like Ctrl-key shortcuts, the SpeedBar allows you to bypass the pull-down menu system to enter commonly used commands more quickly. The SpeedBar is just below the menu bar and contains a series of buttons you can select with the mouse.

Viewing the SpeedBar If you don't have a mouse, the SpeedBar will not be visible.

The available options vary, depending on the mode displayed in the status bar. In Figures 3.4 and 3.5, the SpeedBar is shown in Ready mode and Edit mode.

21

Lesson 3

Figure 3.4   The SpeedBar in READY mode.

Figure 3.5   The SpeedBar in EDIT mode.

Although the SpeedBar options may vary depending on the current activity, the most common options are listed here:

The *Erase, Copy,* and *Move* buttons allow you to delete, copy, and move data from selected cells.

The *Style* button allows you to apply a named style to a selected cell or group of cells.

The *Align* button allows you to align data in a cell flush left, flush right, or centered.

The *Font* button allows you to change the typeface, type size, and color of the selected text, and boldface, italicize, or underline the text.

The *Insert* and *Delete* buttons allow you to insert or delete rows, columns, or a selected block of cells.

The *Fit* button provides a quick way to automatically adjust a column's width to accommodate the width of the widest entry in the column.

The *Sum* button allows you to quickly determine the total sum of all values in two or more cells.

The *Name* button (in Edit mode) lets you name a cell or cells so that you can reference the cells more easily.

Entering Commands in Quattro Pro

The *Calc* button (in Edit mode) calculates the formula on the input line. This is equivalent to pressing the F9 key.

Too Advanced? Don't worry if many of these concepts seem advanced. As you perform specific tasks in later lessons, you'll see how to use the SpeedBar to save time.

In this lesson, you learned how to enter commands in Quattro Pro through pull-down menus, dialog boxes, Ctrl-key shortcuts, and the SpeedBar. In the next lesson, you will learn how to enter labels and values into a worksheet.

Lesson 4

Entering Labels and Values

In this lesson, you'll learn how to enter data into the cells of a worksheet.

Understanding Worksheet Data

To create a worksheet, you need to enter three types of data: labels, values, and formulas. *Labels* consist of text entries, such as entries you would use for column and row headings. *Values* consist of numeric entries and dates. *Formulas* are entries that perform mathematical operations on the values you enter. Figure 4.1 illustrates how the various types of data interact in a spreadsheet.

Enhancing Text Don't worry if your text doesn't look like the text in the figure; you'll learn how to enhance text in Lesson 12.

In this lesson, you will learn how to enter labels and values into a spreadsheet. In Lesson 5, you will learn about formulas.

Entering Labels and Values

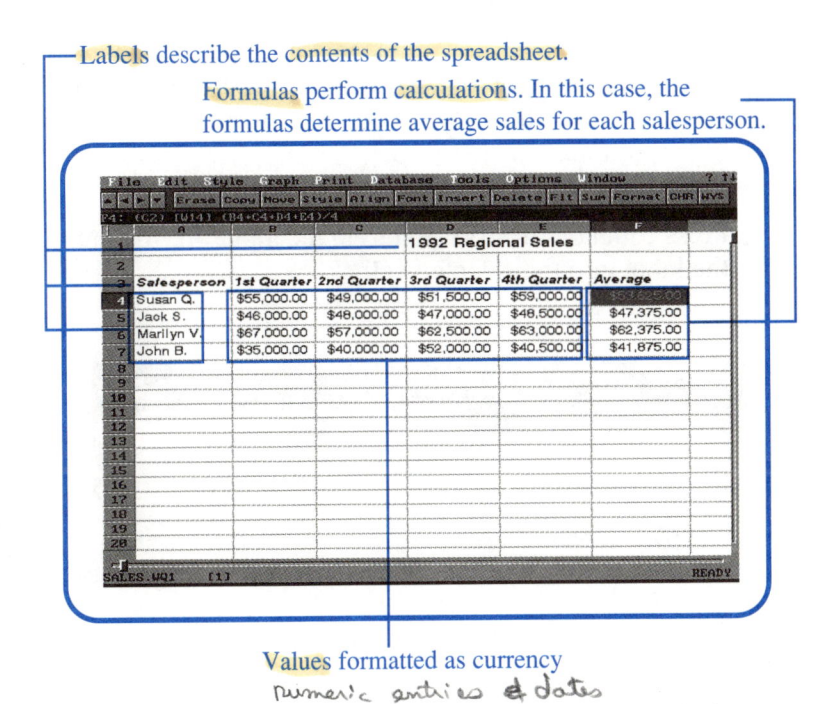

[Figure 4.1 shows a spreadsheet with annotations pointing out:
- Labels describe the contents of the spreadsheet.
- Formulas perform calculations. In this case, the formulas determine average sales for each salesperson.
- Values formatted as currency (numeric entries & dates)

The spreadsheet shows "1992 Regional Sales" with columns: Salesperson, 1st Quarter, 2nd Quarter, 3rd Quarter, 4th Quarter, Average

Salesperson	1st Quarter	2nd Quarter	3rd Quarter	4th Quarter	Average
Susan Q.	$55,000.00	$49,000.00	$51,500.00	$59,000.00	$53,625.00
Jack S.	$46,000.00	$48,000.00	$47,000.00	$48,500.00	$47,375.00
Marilyn V.	$67,000.00	$57,000.00	$62,500.00	$63,000.00	$62,375.00
John B.	$35,000.00	$40,000.00	$52,000.00	$40,500.00	$41,875.00
]

Figure 4.1 A typical spreadsheet contains labels, values, and formulas.

Entering Labels

Labels give your spreadsheet meaning; they indicate what the values in the cells represent. To enter a label, use the following steps:

1. Move the selector to the cell in which you want the label to appear. (Either click inside the cell or use the arrow keys to move the selector.)

2. Type the text you want to use for the label. The text appears on the input line, as shown in Figure 4.2.

25

Lesson 4

Editing Text If you make a mistake, backspace over it and type the correction. In Lesson 10, you will learn other ways of editing information on the input line.

3. Press Enter or click on [Enter] in the input line to enter the label into the selected cell.

Click on [Enter] or press Enter to accept the entry.

Click on [Esc] or press Esc to cancel the entry.

As you type a label, it appears on the Input line.

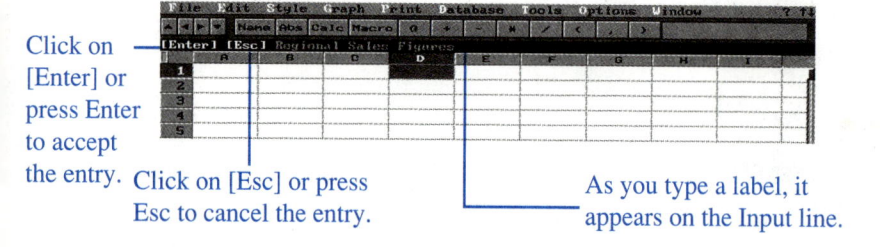

Figure 4.2 Whatever you type appears first on the input line.

Aligning Labels

When you enter a label into a cell, Quattro Pro automatically left aligns the label in the cell. To select an alignment as you enter the label, type one of the following characters before typing the label:

'   Left-aligns the text. (This is the default option. As long as your label starts with a letter, not a number, you do not need to type this character.)

^   Centers the text.

"   Right-aligns the text.

Entering Labels and Values

Defaults A *default* setting is the initial setting for an option. Unless you change the setting, the default is used.

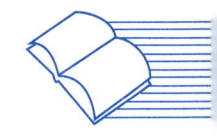

To change the alignment of an existing label, select the cell that contains the label, open the Style menu, and select Alignment. The Alignment submenu appears. Select General, Left, Right, or Center. The General option automatically aligns labels to the left and values to the right.

Bypass the Style Menu To change alignment quickly, press Ctrl-A or click on the Align button in the SpeedBar.

Using Numbers in a Label

If you type any of the following characters as the first character, Quattro Pro will treat the entry as a value or formula instead of as a label:

0 1 2 3 4 5 6 7 8 9 + − . (@ # $

To trick Quattro Pro into treating a numerical entry as a label, precede the entry with one of the alignment characters described in the preceding section. For example, type ' 1992 to have Quattro Pro treat 1992 as a label instead of as a number.

Alignment Characters Don't use alignment characters to align numbers that you want treated as values. To align values, use the Alignment submenu as discussed in the previous section.

27

Lesson 4

Long Entries

If you type a label that's wider than the cell, the label will overlap any empty cells to the right of the current cell (see Figure 4.3). If the cell to the right is not empty, Quattro Pro will display as much of the label as possible in the current cell. In Lesson 11, you will learn how to adjust the width of the columns to accommodate long entries.

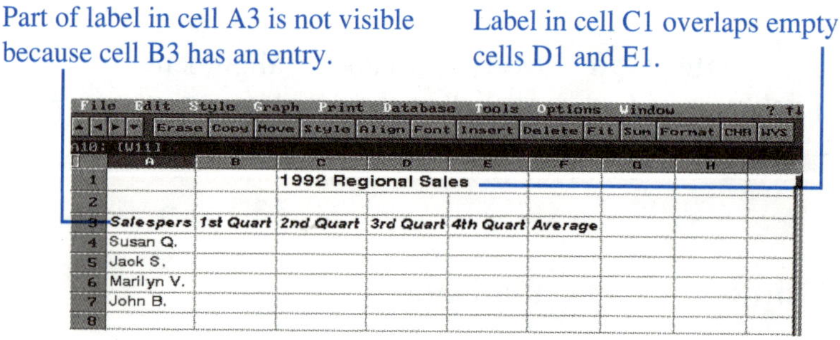

Part of label in cell A3 is not visible because cell B3 has an entry.

Label in cell C1 overlaps empty cells D1 and E1.

Figure 4.3 Quattro Pro lets labels overlap cells if the cells are empty; otherwise, you see only a portion of the entry.

Entering Values

If you start typing an entry with a number, Quattro Pro assumes you are entering a numeric value into the cell. By default, all numeric values are right-justified. To enter a value, take the following steps:

1. Move the selector to the cell in which you want the value to appear.

Entering Labels and Values

2. Type the value. The value appears on the input line. If you make a mistake, backspace over it and type your correction.

3. Press Enter or click on [Enter] in the input line to enter the value into the selected cell.

Long Entries

If you type a value that's wider than the cell, Quattro Pro displays a series of asterisks (*****). You will be able to see the value only on the input line. To have the value appear in the cell, you must widen the column, as explained in Lesson 11.

Formatting Values

Numeric values have little meaning unless they express some unit of measure. For example, 99 can mean 99 percent, 99 dollars, 99 cents, or any other unit. Quattro Pro has a feature which automatically formats your entries for you. For more information, refer to Lesson 12.

Entering Dates

Although you can enter a date as a label, Quattro Pro allows you to enter a date in a special format, which makes it possible to perform mathematical operations on dates. Quattro Pro displays the date in a standard format but inserts a number in the cell. The number represents the number of days that have passed since December 30, 1899.

Lesson 4

You can then use the entry in a formula to calculate future or past dates, such as delivery dates or dates past due. To enter a date, perform the following steps:

1. Move the selector to the cell in which you want the date to appear.

2. Press Ctrl-D and type the date in the form *MM/DD/YY*. For example, type `09/21/92`. The date appears on the input line.

3. Press Enter or click on [Enter] in the input line to enter the date into the selected cell. The date is inserted into the cell in the form MM/DD/YY, but it now appears on the input line as the number of days that have passed since December 30, 1899.

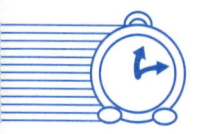

Date Trivia   If you enter a date prior to December 30, 1899, Quattro Pro enters a negative value for the number of days.

In this lesson, you learned how to enter labels and values into cells and how to align labels. In the next lesson, you will learn how to enter formulas that will perform calculations in the spreadsheet.

Lesson 5
Entering Formulas

In this lesson, you'll learn how to enter formulas that perform mathematical operations on values.

Understanding Formulas

Spreadsheets use *formulas* to perform calculations on the data you enter. With formulas, you can perform addition, subtraction, multiplication, or division using the values contained in various cells.

Formulas typically consist of one or more cell addresses and/or values and a mathematical operator, such as + (addition), – (subtraction), * (multiplication), or / (division). For example, if you want to determine the average of the three values contained in cells A1, B1, and C1, and display the answer in cell D1, you would enter the following formula into cell D1:

(A1+B1+C1)/3

Start Right Every formula must begin with one of the following characters:

0 1 2 3 4 5 6 7 8 9 . + – @ # $

31

Lesson 5

Figure 5.1 shows several formulas in action. Table 5.1 lists the mathematical operators you can use to create formulas.

+B16+C16+D16+E16 totals the 4 Quarter profits to determine total profit.
+E10+E11+E12+E13 gives total expenses for 4th Quarter.
+E4+E5+E6 gives total income for 4th Quarter.
+E7-E14 subtracts expenses from income to determine profit.

	A	B	C	D	E	F
1	Hokey Manufacturing					
2						
3	Income	1st Quarter	2nd Quarter	3rd Quarter	4th Quarter	
4	Wholesale	$55,000.00	$46,000.00	$52,000.00	$90,900.00	
5	Retail	$45,700.00	$56,500.00	$42,300.00	$57,900.00	
6	Special Sales	$23,000.00	$25,400.00	$23,300.00	$67,500.00	
7	Total Income	$123,700.00	$127,900.00	$117,600.00	$216,300.00	
8						
9	Expenses					
10	Materials	$19,000.00	$17,500.00	$18,200.00	$20,500.00	
11	Labor	$15,000.00	$15,050.00	$15,500.00	$15,400.00	
12	Rent	$1,600.00	$1,600.00	$1,600.00	$1,600.00	
13	Miscellaneous	$2,500.00	$2,550.00	$3,000.00	$1,500.00	
14	Total Expenses	$38,100.00	$36,700.00	$38,300.00	$39,000.00	
15						Total Profit
16	Profit	$85,600.00	$91,200.00	$79,300.00	$177,300.00	$433,400.00
17						
18						

Figure 5.1 A formula performs the specified calculations and inserts the result.

Table 5.1 Quattro Pro's mathematical operators.

Operator	Performs	Sample Formula	Result
^	Exponentiation	+A1^3	Enters the result of raising the value in cell A1 to the third power.

32

Entering Formulas

Operator	Performs	Sample Formula	Result
+	Addition	+A1+A2	Enters the total of the values in cells A1 and A2.
−	Subtraction	+A1−A2	Subtracts the value in cell A2 from the value in cell A1.
*	Multiplication	+A2*3	Multiplies the value in cell A2 by 3.
/	Division	+A1/50	Divides the value in cell A1 by 50.
	Combination	(A1+A2+A3)/3	Determines the average of the values in cells A1 through A3.

Order of Operations

Quattro Pro performs a series of operations in the following order, giving some operators *precedence* over others:

1st   Exponential equations

2nd   Multiplication and division

3rd   Addition and subtraction

This is important to keep in mind when you are creating equations because the order of operations determines the result.

33

Lesson 5

For example, if you want to determine the average of the values in cells A1, B1, and C1, and you enter `+A1+B1+C1/3`, you'll get the wrong answer. Because division comes before addition in precedence, the value in C1 will be divided by 3, and that result will be added to A1+B1. To determine the total of A1 through C1 first, you must enclose that group of values in parentheses: (A1+B1+C1)/3.

Entering Formulas

You can enter formulas in one of two ways: by *typing* the formula or by *pointing*. The typing method requires you to type the cell addresses used in the formula. Pointing allows you to enter the addresses by clicking on the cells you want to use in the formula. To type a formula, perform the following steps:

1. Move the selector to the cell in which you want the formula to appear.

2. Type `+` or any of the characters required to start a formula.

3. Type the formula, using the necessary cell addresses, values, and mathematical operators.

4. Press Enter or click on [Enter] to accept the formula. Or press Esc or click on [Esc] to cancel the operation.

To enter a formula using the pointing method, take the following steps:

1. Move the selector to the cell in which you want the formula to appear.

Entering Formulas

2. Type + or any of the characters required to start a formula.

3. Click on the cell whose address you want to appear first in the formula. The cell address is inserted to the right of the + sign on the input line.

Keyboard Pointing To point with the keyboard, press F3 and move the selector to the desired cell.

4. Type a mathematical operator after the value to indicate the next operation you want to perform, or click on the operator button in the SpeedBar. The operator appears on the input line.

5. Continue clicking on cells and typing operators until the formula is complete.

6. Press Enter or click on [Enter] to accept the formula. Or press Esc or click on [Esc] to cancel the operation.

Using Absolute Cell References

If you need to use the same formula in several cells in a worksheet, you can save time by copying the contents of the cell, as explained in Lesson 10. When you copy formulas, Quattro Pro adjusts the cell references in the formulas relative to their new positions in the worksheet. For example, in Figure 5.1, cell B7 contains the formula +B4+B5+B6, which determines the total 1st Quarter income. If you copy that formula to cell C7 (to determine the total 2nd Quarter income), Quattro Pro automatically changes the formula to +C4+C5+C6.

35

Lesson 5

However, suppose you want to copy a formula that refers to the same cell in every case. For example, in Figure 5.2, cell C12 contains a formula that multiplies the sales figure in C10 by the overhead percentage in cell C3 to determine the overhead expense. If you were to copy the formula in cell C12 into cell D12, the formula would be +D10*D3, but because there is no entry in cell D3, it would result in an error message. To have each copy of the formula refer to cell C3, you must mark the cell reference as an *absolute* reference.

When a reference is marked as an absolute reference, it remains fixed in any cell into which the formula is copied

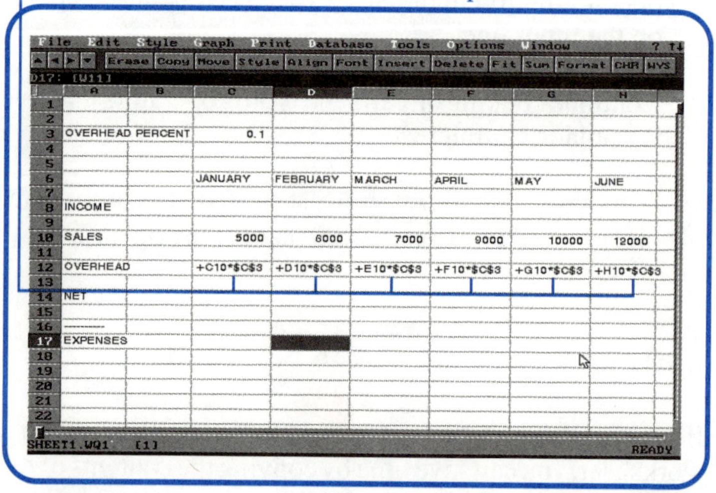

Figure 5.2 If several formulas refer to an entry in the same cell, use absolute references when copying formulas.

To make a cell reference absolute, you add a $ (dollar sign) to the cell address. You can make the row, column, or both as absolute references. For example:

36

Entering Formulas

A1 marks both the column and row as absolute references.

$A1 marks only the column.

A$1 marks only the row.

You can either type the dollar sign(s) on the input line or follow these steps to mark an absolute reference:

1. Move the selector to the cell containing the formula that has the cell references you want to mark as absolute.

2. Press **F2** or click on the input line to put Quattro Pro into Edit mode.

3. Move the cursor to the cell address you want to make absolute.

4. Press **F4**, the Absolute Value key. Pressing it once makes both the column letter and row number of the cell reference absolute. Pressing it again makes only the row reference absolute. Pressing **F4** once more makes only the column reference absolute. Pressing **F4** a fourth time turns Absolute Value off.

Changing the Recalculation Setting

Quattro Pro recalculates the formulas in a worksheet every time you edit a value in a cell. However, on a large worksheet, you may not want Quattro Pro to recalculate until you have entered all your changes. To change the recalculation setting to Manual, use the following steps:

Lesson 5

1. Open the **O**ptions menu.

2. Select **R**ecalculation. The Recalculation submenu appears.

3. Select **M**ode. Three options are presented in the **M**ode submenu:

    Automatic   Automatically recalculates all affected formulas.

    Manual   Recalculates affected formulas when you press **F9**.

    Background   Recalculates all affected formulas between keystrokes. You can continue working while Quattro Pro is recalculating.

4. Select **M**anual. Now Quattro Pro will recalculate the worksheet only when you press **F9**. (If you are in Edit mode, you can recalculate by pressing the **Calc** button in the SpeedBar.)

In this lesson, you learned how to construct formulas by using cell references and mathematical operators. In the next lesson, you will learn how to use Quattro Pro's built-in functions and the new TurboSum feature.

Lesson 6
Entering Functions

In this lesson, you'll learn how to use Quattro Pro's built-in functions and the new TurboSum feature.

Understanding Functions

Functions are complex ready-made formulas that perform a series of operations on a specified *range* of values. For example, if you need to determine the sum of a series of numbers in cells A1 through H1, you can enter the function `@SUM(A1..H1)` instead of entering `+A1+B1+C1+D1+E1+F1+G1+H1`. Appendix A provides a list of commonly used Quattro Pro functions.

Ranges When specifying a range of cells, you can separate the addresses of the first and last cells with one or two periods.

Entering Functions

Every function consists of the following three elements:

Lesson 6

- The @ sign indicates that what follows is a function.

- The *function name* (for example, SUM) indicates the operation that will be performed.

- The *argument* (for example, A1..H1) indicates the cell addresses of the values that the function will act on. The argument is often a range of cells, but it can be much more complex.

Just as with formulas, you can enter a function by either typing or by using the pointing method. To type a function, use the following steps:

1. Move the selector to the cell in which you want the function to appear.

2. Type @ to indicate that you are about to enter a function.

3. Type the function's name followed by the argument in parentheses. For example, type AVG(C5..C25) to calculate the average of the values in cells C5 through C25.

4. Press Enter or click on [Enter] to accept the function. Or Esc or click on [Esc] to cancel the operation.

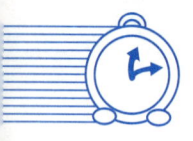

Using the Point Method You can also use the Point method to assemble a function, as you can with formulas (see Lesson 5). After typing @NAME(, use the Point method to specify the range of cells on which you want the function to act.

You can also enter a function by selecting it from the functions list, as shown in Figure 6.1. To display the functions list, move the selection cursor to the cell in which

40

Entering Functions

you want the function to appear, press F2, and then click on the @ button in the SpeedBar, or press Alt-F3. When you select the function you want to use, Quattro Pro inserts the function in the form @NAME(, so you can start typing the argument. Remember to type) at the end of the argument.

Select a function to have it appear on the Input line.

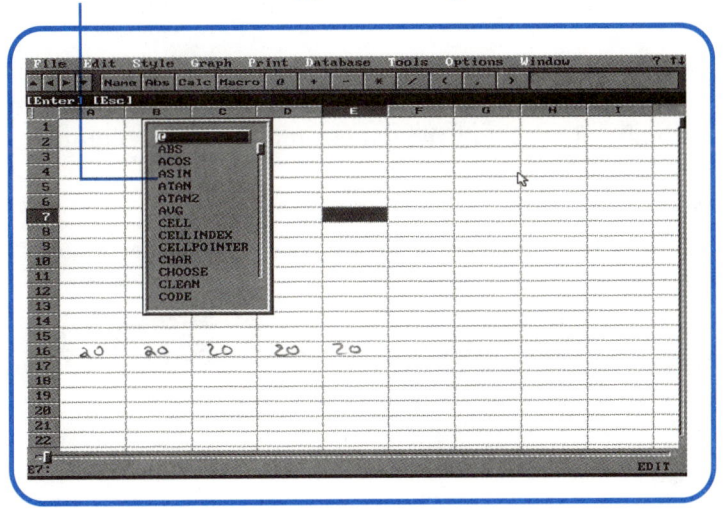

Figure 6.1 You can select a function from the functions list.

Using TurboSum

Because adding a row or column of numbers is the most common operation you'll perform in spreadsheets, Quattro Pro offers a TurboSum feature, which calculates a sum at the press of a button. To use the feature, take the following steps:

41

Lesson 6

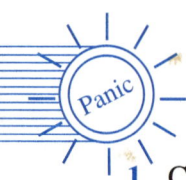

> **Panic**
>
> **Mouse Required** The TurboSum feature requires a mouse.

1. Click inside the first cell that contains a value you want included in the total.

2. Drag the mouse pointer to highlight all the cells you want to total plus one empty cell (see Figure 6.2).

3. Click on the Sum button in the SpeedBar. The TurboSum feature enters a SUM function argument in the empty cell, which totals the values in the row or column.

Select the three cells you want to total...
and the empty cell where you want the total placed.

Figure 6.2 The TurboSum feature lets you quickly total a column or row of values.

42

Error Message? If Quattro Pro displays an error message, you probably forgot to include a blank cell in the block of cells you selected. You must select a blank cell to tell TurboSum where to insert the result.

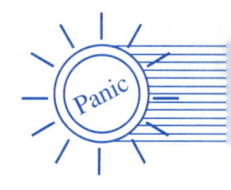

Logical Operators

In addition to mathematical operators, Quattro Pro allows you to use *logical operators*. For example, you can use a logical operator along with the IF function in a sales invoice to determine if a customer has to pay out-of-state sales tax (see Figure 6.3). If the customer's state is specified in cell D17 and the subtotal of the invoice is in cell G29, the statement might read as follows:

@IF(D17=IN,.05*G29,0)

That is, if the state specified in cell D17 is (=) Indiana (IN), then (,), multiply the subtotal in cell G29 by .05 (5%); otherwise, enter 0 for the sales tax. Table 6.1 shows a list of logical operators. For more information on using logical operators, refer to the Quattro Pro documentation.

Table 6.1 Logical operators.

Operator	Meaning
<	Less than
>	Greater than
<=	Less than or equal to
>=	Greater than or equal to

43

Lesson 6

Operator	Meaning
< >	Less than or greater than but not equal to
=	Equal to
#NOT#	Logical NOT
#AND#	Logical AND
#OR#	Logical OR

Because B5 = IN, the value in H17 is multiplied by .05 to determine tax due

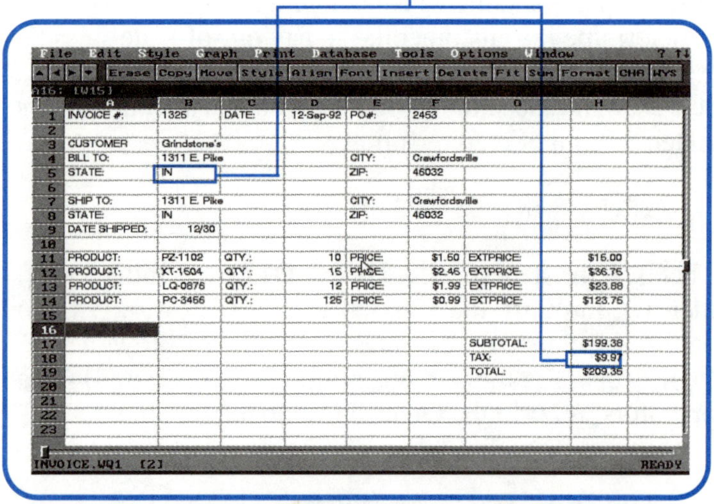

Figure 6.3 You can use logical operators to define a condition.

In this lesson, you learned how to construct formulas by using cell references and logical operators. In the next lesson, you will learn about saving, closing, opening, and retrieving worksheets.

Lesson 7
Saving, Closing, and Opening Worksheets

In this lesson, you'll learn how to save, close, open, and retrieve worksheets.

Saving Worksheets

As you work, the data you enter in a worksheet is stored temporarily in your computer's *Random-Access Memory* (*RAM*). RAM is temporary storage; when the power to your computer is turned off, you lose everything in RAM. That's why you must save worksheets onto disks. The following sections explain the different ways to save worksheets.

Saving a Worksheet for the First Time

When you first start Quattro Pro, the program displays a temporary worksheet named SHEET1.WQ1 with which you can begin working. You can make the worksheet file permanent by saving it to disk under the default name or under a different name.

Lesson 7

DOS File Name Conventions When you save a worksheet, you will be asked to name it. The name consists of a base name (up to eight characters), a period, and an extension (up to three characters). You cannot use any of the following characters:

space ' + = | \ / < > , { }

If you don't type a period and extension, Quattro Pro adds the extension .WQ1 to the file name.

Use the following steps to save a worksheet file:

1. Open the File menu.

2. Select Save. The Save File dialog box appears, as shown in Figure 7.1. The first line reads Enter save file name. Underneath is the path to the directory in which the file will be saved.

3. If you are satisfied with the path that Quattro Pro has chosen, type a name for the file and press Enter. To change the path, press Esc twice to erase the path, and then type a path and file name. For example, to save the file as SALES.WQ1 in the directory C:\QPRO\DATA, type c:\qpro\data\sales and press Enter.

Dialog Box Command Buttons You can use the command buttons on the right side of the dialog box to change drives, to move up the directory tree, or to change the list display (see Figure 7.1). To select one of these buttons with the keyboard, press /, use the arrow keys to switch to the button, and press Enter.

Saving, Closing, and Opening Worksheets

To move down the directory tree, choose a subdirectory from the list.

Click here to enlarge the file list.

Click here to move up one directory.

Click here for more information about the files.

Click here to change drives.

Click here to select from a list of previously opened files.

Click here to change to a network drive.

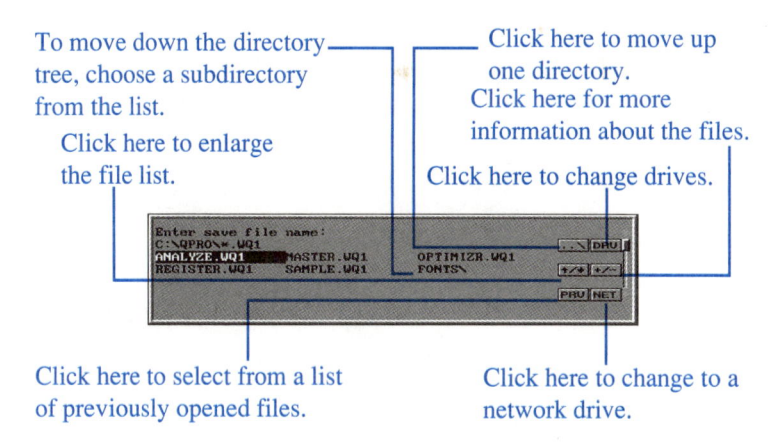

Figure 7.1   The Save File dialog box.

Path   The path tells Quattro Pro where the file is located. A path is expressed in the form *c:\maindir\subdir\subdir*, where *c* represents the letter of the drive, *maindir* represents the name of the directory, and *subdir* represents the name of any subdirectories under the main directory. (The directory must exist before you can save a file to it.)

Saving an Existing Worksheet to Disk

As you modify the worksheet data, you should save the worksheet to disk every 10 to 15 minutes to protect your data. Use the following steps to save an existing worksheet:

1. Open the **File** menu and select **Save**. A dialog box appears telling you that the file already exists.

2. Select **Replace** to replace the file on disk with the new file, select **Backup** to create a backup file, or select **Cancel** to cancel the save operation.

47

Lesson 7

Save All If you have more than one worksheet open, select Save All from the File menu to save all the worksheets. Quattro Pro will display a dialog box for each worksheet, prompting you to confirm the save operation.

Saving a Worksheet Under Another Name

Quattro Pro's **F**ile menu contains a Save **A**s command, which allows you to create a copy of a worksheet file. This is useful if you want to create a copy of the worksheet and change the copy without affecting the original file. To create a copy, take the following steps:

1. Open the File menu and select Save As.

2. Type a different name for the file and press Enter.

Closing a Worksheet File

When you save a worksheet, it remains on-screen. Closing a worksheet file removes it from the screen. Be sure to save your work before you use the following steps to close a worksheet:

1. Open the File menu.

2. Select Close. If you have made changes to the worksheet since the last time you saved it, a dialog box appears asking, Lose your changes?

3. If the dialog box appears, select Yes to close the worksheet without saving any changes, or select No to close the dialog box and return to the worksheet.

Saving, Closing, and Opening Worksheets

Close All If you have more than one worksheet open, select Close All from the File menu to close all the worksheets. If you made changes to any of the worksheets since the last time you saved, Quattro Pro will display a dialog box for each worksheet, asking if you want to lose the changes.

Opening or Retrieving a Worksheet

Once you've saved a worksheet to disk, you can open or retrieve the worksheet at any time. If you *open* a worksheet, Quattro Pro opens a separate window for the file. If you *retrieve* a worksheet, Quattro Pro retrieves the file into the current window, replacing any data in the window with data from the file.

To open or retrieve a worksheet file, use the following steps:

1. Open the File menu and select Open or Retrieve. If you choose Open, the Open File dialog box appears, as shown in Figure 7.1.

2. If you choose Retrieve, a dialog box may appear, asking if you want to lose changes in the current worksheet. Choose Yes to lose the changes, or choose No, save the file, and start over at step 1.

3. Type a complete path to the drive and directory that contains the file you want to retrieve or open. For example, type `c:\qpro\data` and press Enter. Quattro Pro displays a list of all files in that directory that have the .WQ1 extension.

49

Lesson 7

4. Highlight the name of the file you want to open or retrieve and press Enter, or double-click on the name of the file. Quattro Pro opens the worksheet file in a separate window.

File Not Listed? If the file you want to open is not listed, you may have saved the file using an extension other than .WQ1. Try typing *.* to view all the files in the selected directory.

Switching Windows

You can have more than one worksheet open at a time (depending on the amount of free memory); Quattro Pro displays each worksheet in a separate window. To switch between windows, take the following steps:

1. Open the Window menu and select Pick or press Alt-0. A list of open worksheet files appears.

2. Select a worksheet from the list.

The **Window menu also contains options that allow** you to **Tile or Stack the windows**, **M**ove/Size the active window, or **Z**oom in on a window. (The **S**tack and **M**ove/Size options do not work in **WYSIWYG mode.**)

In this lesson, you learned how to save worksheet files to disk, how to close worksheets, and how to open and retrieve worksheets. In the next lesson, you will learn how to select cells and cell blocks in order to work with them.

Lesson 8
Selecting Cell Blocks

In this lesson, you will learn how to select a range of cells in order to work with the cells as a group.

Cells and Cell Blocks

In previous lessons, you selected individual cells in order to enter labels, values, formulas, and functions. In this lesson, you will learn how to select a *range* of cells in order to copy, move, erase the cells, name the range of cells, or format the cells as a group.

Range A range defines a rectangular block of cells using the cell addresses of the cells in the upper left and lower right corners, of the cell block. In Figure 8.1, for example, the range of cells is C3..F10.

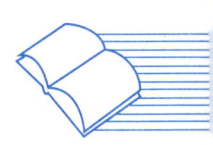

Selecting a Cell Block

Selecting a cell block allows you to perform the same operation on several cells at the same time. For example, you can move or delete several cells, change the character formatting in the cells, or perform a mathematical operation on a group of cells.

51

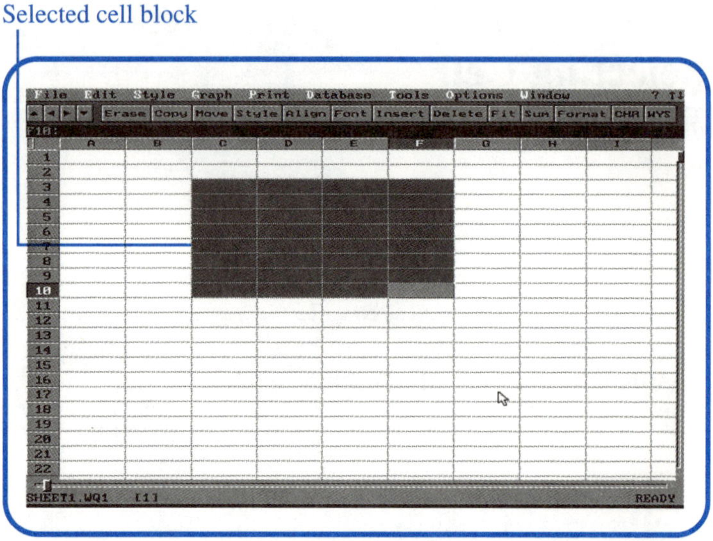

Figure 8.1 A cell block is defined by the cells in the upper left and lower right corners of the block.

The procedure for selecting a cell block depends on whether you are using the keyboard or the mouse, as explained in the following sections.

Selecting with the Mouse

With the mouse, you can select a block by dragging the mouse pointer over the cells. Use the following steps to select a block of cells using your mouse:

1. Move the mouse pointer to the first cell in the block.

2. Hold down the left mouse button and drag the mouse pointer to the last cell in the block.

Selecting with the Keyboard

With the keyboard, you can select a block of cells by *anchoring* the selector in one cell and extending the selection over the desired cells. To extend the selection, perform the following steps:

1. Move the selector to the first or last cell in the block you want to select.

2. Press Shift-F7. EXT appears in the status line, indicating that you are now in Extend mode.

3. Use the arrow keys to stretch the highlight over the cells you want to include in the block.

4. Press F7 to turn off Extend mode.

Quickly Selecting a Cell Block To quickly extend the selection in a row or column, move the selector to the first or last cell in the block, press Shift-F7, and then press End and an arrow key. You can also extend the selection by clicking on one of the arrow buttons in the SpeedBar or Mouse Palette.

Specifying a Range of Cells

You will often enter commands in Quattro Pro that prompt you to specify a *range* of cells. For example, if you select Copy from the Edit menu, a prompt appears on the input line asking you to specify the range of cells you want to copy. The box may contain an entry such as A11..A11, which you can either accept or edit. The mode indicator indicates you are in POINT mode. You can either type the range on the input line or select the range by using the arrow keys or the mouse.

53

Lesson 8

Typing a Range

To specify a range of cells by typing an entry, you must type an entry that specifies the first cell and the last cell in the block. For example, the entry D10..D14 specifies the cell block shown in Figure 8.2. (You can use either one or two periods to separate the cell addresses in an entry.)

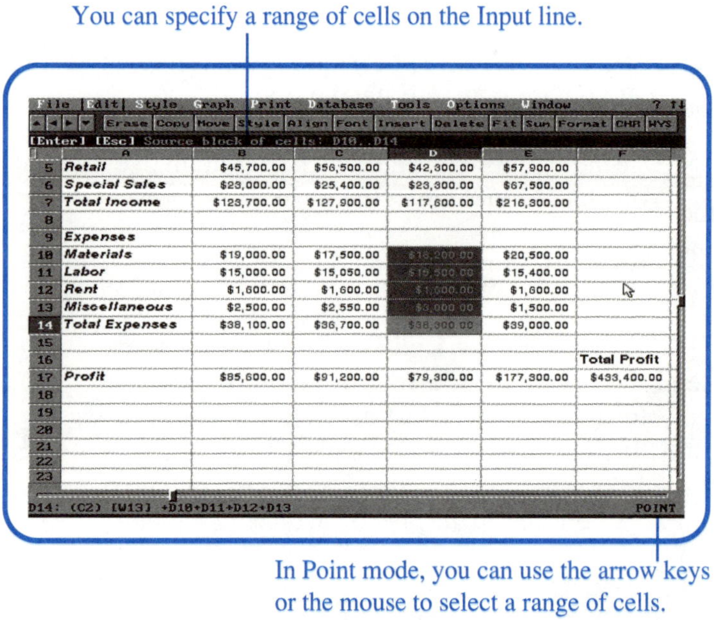

You can specify a range of cells on the Input line.

In Point mode, you can use the arrow keys or the mouse to select a range of cells.

Figure 8.2. You can type a range to specify a block of cells.

Using the Point Method

To use the Point method, you must be in Point mode; POINT must be displayed on the status line. Quattro Pro automati-

54

cally enters Point mode when you select certain options, such as Copy, Move, or Erase.

In Point mode, you can select a range of cells by performing the following steps:

1. Move the selection cursor to the cell in the upper left corner of the block you want to select.

Anchoring the Highlight   With some options, Quattro Pro automatically anchors the highlight in the current cell. You can extend the highlight over a cell block by pressing the arrow keys. In other cases, you can move the selector without extending the highlight; then you must manually anchor the selector. To remove the anchoring, press Esc.

2. Press . (period) to anchor the selector in the current cell.

3. Use the arrow keys to extend the selection to the remaining cells.

4. Press Enter or click on [Enter].

Selecting with the Mouse   In Point mode, you can select a cell block with your mouse by dragging the mouse pointer over the cells you want to select. Click on [Enter] after selecting the cells.

In this lesson, you learned how to select multiple cells. In the next lesson, you will learn how to name individual cells and cell blocks in order to make working with them more logical.

Lesson 9

Naming Cells and Ranges

In this lesson, you'll learn how to name cells and ranges so that you can use names instead of cell addresses to work with cells and cell blocks.

Using Named Cells and Ranges

In Lesson 5, you learned how to use cell addresses to construct formulas. A more logical way to construct formulas (and to work with blocks of cells) is to use *cell names*. For example, say you want to determine your net income by subtracting expenses from income. You can name the cell that contains your total income INCOME, and name the cell that contains your total expenses EXPENSES. You can then determine your net income by using the formula:

+INCOME–EXPENSES

to make the formula more logical and easier to manage.

Naming cells and ranges also makes it easier to cut, copy, and move blocks of cells, as explained in Lesson 10.

Naming Cells and Ranges

Naming a Cell

To assign a name to a cell, use the following steps:

1. Select the cell you want to name.

2. Open the Edit menu and select Names.

3. Select Create. The Create Names dialog box appears, as shown in Figure 9.1.

4. Type a name for the cell and press Enter, or click on the Enter button. A prompt appears on the input line asking you to specify the cell block to name.

5. Press Enter or click on [Enter] to name only the current cell.

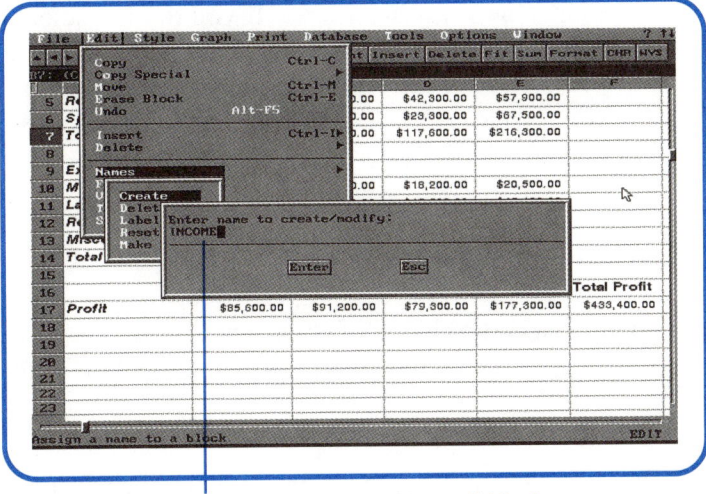

Type a name for the cell or cell block.

Figure 9.1 The Create Names dialog box prompts you to enter a name for the cell.

57

Lesson 9

Naming a Range

The process for naming a range of cells is basically the same, except you have to select a block of cells before or after naming the range:

1. Select the block of cells you want to name. Refer to Lesson 8 if you don't know how to select a block of cells.

2. Open the Edit menu and select Names.

3. Select Create. The Create Names dialog box appears (see Figure 9.1).

4. Type a name for the cell block and press Enter, or click on the Enter button.

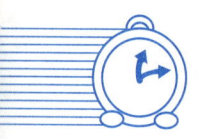

> **Using the Point Method**   If you did not select a block of cells before closing Edit/Names/Create, you could use the Point method as discussed in the previous lesson to select the cells.

Finding Cells by Their Names

If you name a cell or block of cells, you can use the name to quickly find the cell(s) using Quattro Pro's GoTo key (F5):

1. Press F5. The input line prompts you to specify a cell address.

2. Type the name of the cell or cell block.

Naming Cells and Ranges

3. Press Enter or click on [Enter]. The selector moves to the cell or to the first cell in the block.

Making a Table of Cell Names

As you name several cells and/or cell blocks, it becomes easy to forget the exact names and their ranges. Quattro Pro offers a handy way to keep this information at your fingertips—a table of cell names. To create such a table, perform the following steps:

1. Open the Edit menu.

2. Select Names.

3. Select Make Table. Quattro Pro prompts you to specify the cells where you want the table inserted.

4. Position the cell pointer in a portion of the worksheet where it will not overwrite any existing data and press Enter or click on [Enter].

Quattro Pro returns you to the worksheet and inserts the table of cell names. The table consists of two columns: the first contains the names; the second, the cell addresses.

In this lesson, you learned how to name cells and ranges to create a more logical spreadsheet. In the next lesson, you will learn how to edit the contents of cells and cut, copy, and move individual cells or groups of cells.

Lesson 10
Editing Cells

In this lesson, you'll learn how to edit the contents of cells and erase, copy, and move individual cells or groups of cells.

Editing the Contents of a Cell

Once you've entered a label, value, or formula in a cell, you can replace the entry or edit it. To replace the entry, select the cell, type the new entry, and press Enter. To edit the entry, use the following steps:

1. Select the cell whose contents you want to edit.

2. Press F2 or click on the input line. The contents of the cell appear on the input line followed by a cursor, as shown in Figure 10.1.

3. Use the keys listed in Table 10.1 to edit the entry.

4. Press Enter or click on [Enter] on the left side of the input line to accept the entry, or press Esc or click on [Esc] twice to cancel.

Editing Cells

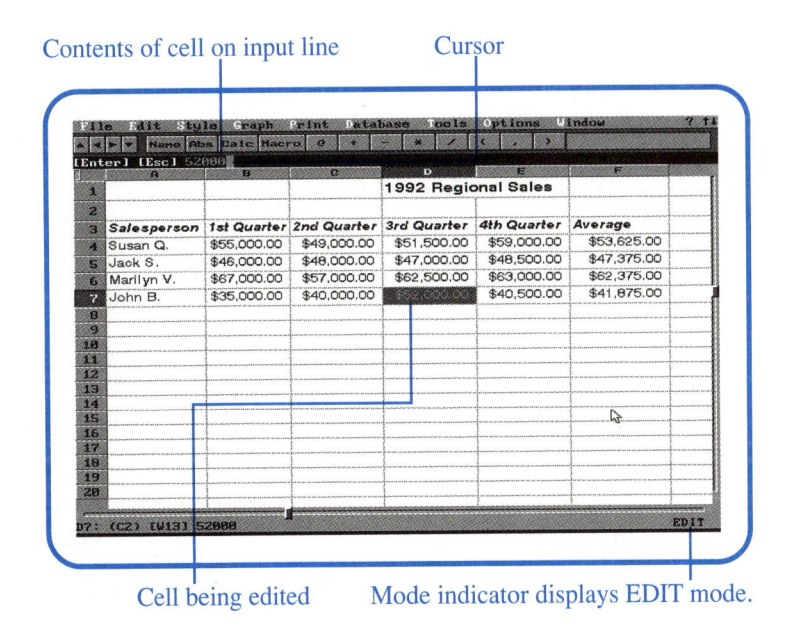

Figure 10.1 You can edit the cell's contents on the input line.

(Labels: Contents of cell on input line; Cursor; Cell being edited; Mode indicator displays EDIT mode.)

Table 10.1 The Quattro Pro edit keys.

Press	To
←, →	Move the cursor left or right one character.
Home	Move the cursor to the beginning of the input line.
End	Move the cursor to the end of the input line.
Tab	Move the cursor right five characters.
Shift-Tab	Move the cursor left five characters.
Del	Delete the character the cursor is on.
Backspace	Delete the character to the left of the cursor.

61

Deleting Cell Contents

If you need to clear data from cells, you can delete the cells' contents by performing the following steps:

1. Select the cell or cells whose contents you want to delete.

2. Open the Edit menu and select Erase Block.

Quattro Pro deletes the contents of the cells. Any formatting remains intact.

Quickly Deleting a Cell's Contents To delete the contents of a cell or cells, select the cell(s) and press the Del key or Ctrl-E.

Insert and Overstrike

By default, when you type text on the input line, whatever you type is inserted at the cursor location. Any existing text is shifted to the right to accommodate the new text. If you want to type over existing text rather than insert text, you can switch to *Overstrike mode*. To switch modes, press the Ins (Insert) key on your keyboard. When you are in Overstrike mode, you'll see OVR on the right side of the status line.

Copying the Contents and Formatting of Cells

The Copy and Copy Special commands allow you to copy the contents and/or formatting (such as shading) of selected

Editing Cells

cell(s) to another area on the spreadsheet. The Copy command is useful for entering duplicate entries in a different set of cells. The difference between Copy and Copy Special is that the Copy command copies both the contents of a cell *and* its formatting, whereas Copy Special copies either the contents *or* the formatting. To copy cells, perform these steps:

1. Select the cell or cells whose contents you want to copy.

2. Open the Edit menu and select Copy. If you selected only one cell, press Enter or click on [Enter] to confirm that it's the only cell you want to copy. The input line prompts you to select the destination for the copied cells, as shown in Figure 10.2.

Source and Destination Blocks The *source* block contains the cell or cells that you want to copy. The *destination* block is where you want the cell or cells to be copied to.

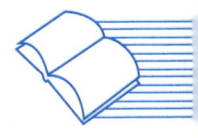

3. Move the selector to the cell in the upper left corner of the destination block. (Make sure there are enough empty cells to the right of or below the cell to hold the copied cells. Otherwise, the copies will overwrite any cells that contain data.)

4. Press Enter or click on [Enter].

Copying Quickly To copy selected cells, click on the Copy button on the left end of the SpeedBar or press Ctrl-C.

Lesson 10

	A	B	C	D	E	F
1				1992 Regional Sales		
2						
3	Salesperson	1st Quarter	2nd Quarter	3rd Quarter	4th Quarter	Average
4	Susan Q.	$55,000.00	$49,000.00	$51,500.00	$59,000.00	$53,625.00
5	Jack S.	$46,000.00	$48,000.00	$47,000.00	$48,500.00	$47,375.00
6	Marilyn V.	$67,000.00	$57,000.00	$62,500.00	$63,000.00	$62,375.00
7	John B.	$35,000.00	$40,000.00	$52,000.00	$40,500.00	$41,875.00

This Input line prompts you to specify a destination for the copied cells.

Figure 10.2 Quattro Pro prompts you to specify a destination for the copied cells.

Moving a Cell Block

If you want to change the location of a block of cells, use Quattro Pro's Move command to relocate the whole block of cells at once. When you move a cell block, it overwrites any information in the destination cells.

Perform the following steps to move a cell block:

1. Select the cell or cells you want to move.

2. Open the Edit menu and choose Move, or click on the Move button in the SpeedBar. If you selected only one cell, press Enter to confirm that it's the only cell you want to move. The input line prompts you to select the destination for the moved cells.

3. Move the selector to the cell in the upper left corner of the destination block.

4. Press Enter or click on [Enter]. Quattro Pro moves the source block data to the destination block.

Editing Cells

Moving Shortcut   Press Ctrl-M to access the **M**ove command quickly.

Undoing Changes

Whenever you change the contents of a cell, erase a cell or cell block, copy cells, move cells, or enter any other change, you have the option of undoing that change. But the Undo feature must be enabled and you must undo the change immediately. To enable the Undo feature, perform the following steps:

1. Open the Options menu and select Other.

2. Select Undo.

3. Select Enable.

4. To turn the feature on permanently, select Update from the Options menu.

5. Select Quit. The Undo feature is now enabled.

To undo a change, open the Edit menu and select Undo, or press Alt-F5. The operation is undone. You can select the Undo option again to undo the Undo operation.

Keeping the Undo feature activated slightly reduces the speed at which Quattro Pro functions. However, it's a good idea to keep this option on.

In this lesson, you learned how to edit cells and how to copy and move the contents of a cell or cell block from one area of the spreadsheet to another. In the next lesson, you will learn how to control rows and columns.

Lesson 11

Controlling Columns and Rows

In this lesson, you'll learn how to widen columns, insert a row or column, delete a row or column, and change the row height.

Changing Column Width

If you enter a value (or if a formula calculates a value) that is too wide for the cell it is in, Quattro Pro displays a series of asterisks in place of the value, as shown in Figure 11.1. If you type a label that is too wide for the cell, Quattro Pro spills the overflow into the next cell (if it's empty) or displays only part of the label. In either case, you'll need to widen the column in order to display the label or value in its proper format.

Calculated values are wider than cells.

Figure 11.1 If a column is too narrow for the contents of the cells, you won't see all your data.

66

Controlling Columns and Rows

To widen a column, perform these steps:

1. Move the selector to any cell in the column you want to widen.

2. Open the Style menu and select Column Width. The input line displays the message Alter the width of the current column [1..254], followed by a value that indicates the current width.

3. Type the number of characters wide you want the column to be or press → to widen the column one character at a time. (Pressing ← reduces the column width.)

4. Press Enter or click on [Enter]. Quattro Pro adjusts the column width and displays values instead of asterisks in cells.

You can reset the column width at any time by choosing Reset Width from the Style menu.

Shortcut Pressing Ctrl-W accesses the Column Width command quickly.

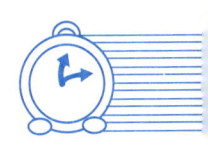

Dragging Column Width You can use your mouse to widen a column. First, move the mouse pointer over the column letter at the top of the column you want to widen. Press and hold down the mouse button, and drag the pointer to the right to increase column width or to the left to decrease the width.

Lesson 11

You can use the **A**uto Width feature to have Quattro Pro make the column as wide as it needs to be to display the widest entry. Quattro Pro will automatically adjust the column width as needed. To turn **Auto Width** on for a selected block of cells, perform the following steps:

1. Select the cells for which you want to turn on **A**uto Width.

2. Open the **S**tyle menu and choose **B**lock Size.

3. Choose **A**uto **W**idth.

4. Type the number of extra spaces you want inserted between the columns, if desired, and press **E**nter or click on [Enter].

Quick Fit   To turn on Auto Width for a block of cells, select the cells and click on the **F**it button in the SpeedBar.

To change the default column width for the entire worksheet, take the following steps:

1. Open the **O**ptions menu and select **F**ormats.

2. Select **G**lobal **W**idth.

3. Type the column width (in number of characters) or use the arrow keys to set the width, and press **E**nter or click on [Enter].

4. Select **Q**uit.

5. To make the setting the default for all worksheets, select **U**pdate.

Controlling Columns and Rows

6. Select **Quit**.

Changing Row Height

Whenever you type an entry in a cell, Quattro Pro automatically sets the row height to accommodate the entry. You can, however, change the row height. Figure 11.2 shows a worksheet with the height of row 1 increased to 26 *points*.

Point Size Row height is usually measured in points. A point is 1/72 of an inch.

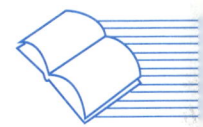

26-point row height

Figure 11.2 A worksheet with the height of row 1 increased to 26 points.

To modify the row height, perform these steps:

1. Move the selector to any cell in the row whose height you want to change.

2. Open the **Style** menu and select **Block Size**.

3. Select **Height**.

4. Select **Set Row Height**.

69

Lesson 11

5. To modify a single row, press Enter or click on [Enter] and type a point size from 1 to 240, or use ↑ or ↓ to set the height. To modify several rows, use ↑ and ↓ to extend the highlight over the rows you want to modify and press Enter. Then enter a point size from 1 to 240 or use the arrow keys to set the height.

6. Press Enter or click on [Enter]. The row height is adjusted.

Dragging Row Height In WYSIWYG mode, you can use your mouse to change the row height. First, move the mouse pointer over the row number at the left of the row whose height you want to change. Press and hold down the mouse button, and drag the pointer down to increase row height or up to decrease the height.

Inserting a Row or Column

While creating a spreadsheet, you may leave out a row or column unintentionally. Because this problem happens so often, Quattro Pro contains a feature that lets you insert a row or column anywhere in the spreadsheet, without damaging any cell references you previously entered. If you insert a row or column within a block that is used in a formula, Quattro Pro adjusts the cell references in the formula to include the new column or row. For example, if the block address is C1..C10 and you insert a new row at row 5, the new block address becomes C1..C11.

When you insert a column, an entire column is inserted to the left of the current column. When you insert a row, an entire row is inserted above the current row.

If you insert a *row block* or a *column block,* you can insert a partial row or column. That is, instead of inserting a row that extends across the entire spreadsheet, you can insert a row that's only a few columns wide, as shown in Figure 11.3. Inserting a row block shifts the contents of the current cells down, whereas inserting a column block shifts the contents to the right.

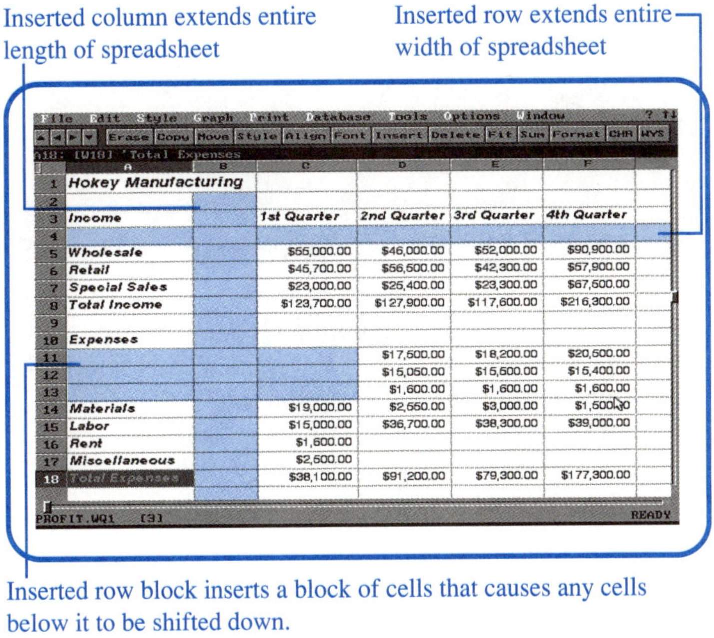

Inserted column extends entire length of spreadsheet

Inserted row extends entire width of spreadsheet

Inserted row block inserts a block of cells that causes any cells below it to be shifted down.

Figure 11.3 You can insert an entire row or column, or a partial row or column.

To insert a row or column, perform these steps:

1. Move the selector to the row beneath or the column to the right of where you want to insert a row or column.

Lesson 11

2. Open the Edit menu and select Insert, or click on the Insert button in the SpeedBar. The Insert Rows or Columns submenu appears.

3. Select Rows, Columns, Row Block, or Column Block.

4. To insert a single row or column, press Enter. To insert multiple rows or columns, use ↑, ↓, ←, and → to extend the highlight and then press Enter or click on [Enter].

> **Shortcut** Pressing Ctrl-I accesses the Insert Rows or Columns submenu quickly.

Deleting Rows or Columns

When you delete a row or column, Quattro Pro adjusts the cell references in any formulas automatically. However, be careful when using the Delete option so that you do not cut off a block used as part of a formula calculation.

To delete a row or column:

1. Move the selector to the row or column you want to delete.

2. Open the Edit menu and select Delete, or click on the Delete button in the SpeedBar.

3. Select Rows, Columns, Row Block, or Column Block.

4. To delete a single row or column, press Enter or click on [Enter]. To delete several rows or columns, use the arrow keys to extend the highlight and press Enter and click on [Enter].

Lesson 12
Enhancing the Appearance of Labels and Values

In this lesson, you'll learn how to format values, change fonts, and align text in cells.

Formatting Values

Numeric values are usually more than just numbers. They represent a dollar value, a date, a percent, or some other real value. To indicate what values represent, you must display the value in a certain format. Quattro Pro offers a wide range of formats, as listed in Table 12.1.

Table 12.1 Value formats.

Format	Description	Example
Fixed	Displays numbers with a fixed number of decimal places, 0-15.	–234.00 234.8431 78.343201
Scientific	Displays numbers in exponential format, including decimal places from 0-15.	–1.6E+9 666E+02 6.66E+09
Currency	Displays numbers in currency format, including a dollar sign and decimal places from 0-15.	$999.90 $99,999,999.00 ($666.00)

continues

Lesson 12

Table 12.1 continued

Format	Description	Example
Comma	Displays numbers including commas to separate thousands; negative values appear in parentheses.	99,999.00 (999)
General	Displays numbers without formatting.	−456 645879 29800
+/−	Converts numbers to horizontal bar graphs; either plus (+) for positive values or minus signs (−) for negative values.	++++ −−−−−
Percent	Displays numbers as a percentage, including decimal places from 0-15.	34.89% 9.98% 11.00%
Date	Displays dates in one of the following formats: 1-(DD-MMM-YY) Day-Month-Year 16-Mar-92 2-(DD-MMM) Day-Month 16-Mar 3-(MMM-YY) Month-Year Mar-92 4-(Long intl.) Long international format 03/16/92 5-(Short intl.) Short international format 03/16	
Time	Displays times in one of the following formats: 1-hh:mm:ss AM/PM 12:24:55 AM 2-hh:mm AM/PM 12:24 AM 3-Long intl. 13:20:33 4-Short intl. 14:55	
Text	Displays formulas instead of values.	+C7−C8
Hidden	Hides the cell contents.	

Enhancing the Appearance of Labels and Values

To format a value, use the following steps:

1. Select the cell(s) that contain the value(s) you want to format.

2. Open the Style menu and select Numeric Format, or click on the Format button in the SpeedBar. The Numeric Format submenu appears, as shown in Figure 12.1.

3. Select the format you want to use. You return to the worksheet, and the value is formatted as specified.

Numeric Format submenu

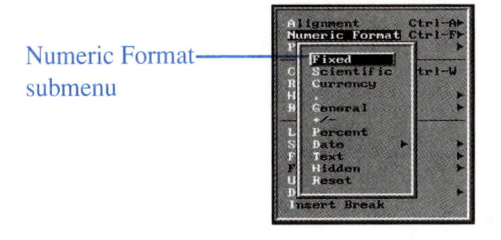

Figure 12.1 Use the Numeric Format submenu to give values meaning.

Quick Value Formatting You can bypass the Style pull-down menu by pressing Ctrl-F to display the Numeric Format submenu.

Changing Fonts

When you enter a label or value, Quattro Pro uses a default *font* for the text. You can change the font to improve the overall appearance of the text or to set the text apart from

75

Lesson 12

other text. The font change affects all characters in the cell; you cannot change fonts within a cell.

What's a font? A font is a set of characters which have the same typeface and point size. For example, Helvetica 12-point is a font. Helvetica is the typeface, and 12-point is the size. (There are approximately 72 points in an inch.) When you select a font, Quattro Pro also allows you to add an *attribute* to the font, such as bold, italic, or underline.

To change fonts, perform the following steps:

1. Select the cell(s) that contain the text whose font you want to change.

2. Open the Style menu and select Font, or click on the Font button in the SpeedBar. If you selected only one cell, press Enter or click on [Enter] to confirm the selection. The Font submenu appears, as shown in Figure 12.2.

3. To change the typeface, select Typeface and choose a typeface from the submenu that appears.

4. To change the size of the type, select Point Size and choose a point size from the submenu that appears.

5. To change the color of the text (if you have a color printer), select Color and choose a color from the menu that appears.

6. To add an attribute to the font, select Bold, Italic, and/or Underlined. (You can add more than one attribute.)

Enhancing the Appearance of Labels and Values

7. Choose **Q**uit to apply the selected font. You are returned to the worksheet, and the text is formatted as specified.

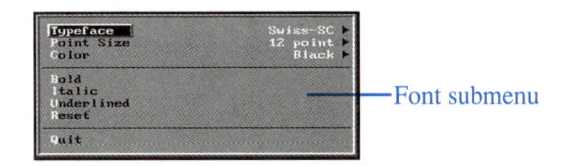

```
Typeface              Swiss-SC ▶
Point Size            12 point ▶
Color                   Black ▶
Bold
Italic
Underlined
Reset
Quit
```
—Font submenu

Figure 12.2 Use the Font submenu to select a typeface, type size, color, and optional attributes.

Quick Fonts The Font **T**able command on the **S**tyle menu opens a submenu that contains a list of commonly used fonts, as shown in Figure 12.3. You can edit this submenu to include only the fonts you use most often, and you can assign attributes to the fonts. Whenever you want to use one of these customized font/attribute combinations, simply select the font from this list.

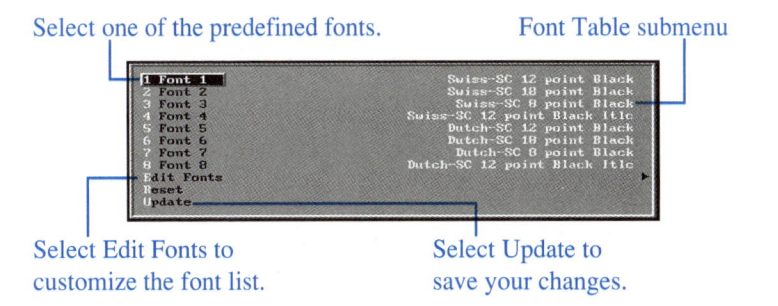

Select one of the predefined fonts.   Font Table submenu

```
1 Font 1              Swiss-SC 12 point Black
2 Font 2              Swiss-SC 18 point Black
3 Font 3              Swiss-SC 8 point Black
4 Font 4         Swiss-SC 12 point Black Itlc
5 Font 5              Dutch-SC 12 point Black
6 Font 6              Dutch-SC 18 point Black
7 Font 7              Dutch-SC 8 point Black
8 Font 8         Dutch-SC 12 point Black Itlc
Edit Fonts                                   ▶
Reset
Update
```

Select Edit Fonts to   Select Update to
customize the font list.   save your changes.

Figure 12.3 The Font Table submenu contains a list of several common font/attribute combinations.

77

Lesson 12

Aligning Text in Cells

By default, Quattro Pro uses General alignment to align labels and values in cells; all labels are left-justified and numbers are right-justified. You can change the alignment at any time by performing the following steps:

1. Select the cell(s) whose alignment you want to change.

2. Open the Style menu and select Alignment, or click on the Align button in the SpeedBar. The Alignment submenu appears, as shown in Figure 12.4.

> **Quick Alignment** For quick access to the Alignment submenu, press Ctrl-A.

3. Select an alignment option. You return to the worksheet, and the contents of the cell(s) are aligned as specified.

Alignment options

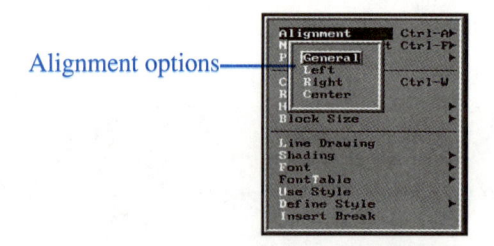

Figure 12.4 Use the Alignment submenu to align the contents of the selected cell(s).

78

Enhancing the Appearance of Labels and Values

Protecting Cell Contents

Quattro Pro allows you to protect a cell or cell block to prevent you or another user from changing the contents of a cell accidentally. To protect cells, perform the following steps:

1. Select the cell(s) you want to protect.

2. Open the Style menu and choose Protection. The Protection submenu appears.

3. Choose Protect. If you selected only one cell, press Enter to confirm the selection.

You can turn protection off by selecting the cells and choosing Unprotect from the Protection submenu.

In this lesson, you learned how to enhance the appearance of a cell's contents by adding a numeric format and by changing fonts and attributes. In the next lesson, you will learn how to add lines and shading to cells and cell blocks.

Lesson 13

Adding Lines and Shading to Cells and Blocks

In this lesson, you'll learn how to enhance your spreadsheet by adding lines and shading to cells or cell blocks.

Drawing Lines Around and Between Cells

If you turned grid lines on (**W**indow/**O**ptions/**G**rid Lines/**D**isplay), border lines appear around each cell to help you identify it. When you print the spreadsheet, however, no lines are printed. To have lines appear on the printout, you must specify where you want the lines to appear and the type of line you want to use. Figure 13.1 shows the options for adding lines to cells and cell blocks.

To draw lines around or between cells, perform the following steps:

1. Select the cell or cell block where you want the lines to appear.

2. Open the Style menu and select Line Drawing. If you selected only one cell, press Enter or click on [Enter] to confirm the selection. The Line Drawing Placement submenu appears (see Figure 13.2).

Adding Lines and Shading to Cells and Blocks

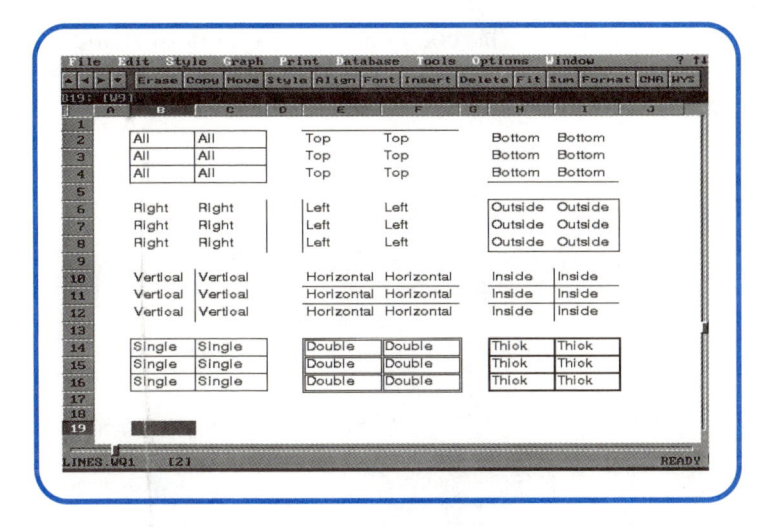

Figure 13.1 Line drawing options.

3. Select a line placement option from the Placement list. The Line Types submenu appears.

4. Select a line type from the Line Types submenu. You return to the worksheet, and the selected line type appears around the specified cell(s).

5. You remain in Line Draw mode. To place lines around and between other cells, simply select the cells, press Enter, and select a placement and line type option.

6. Press Esc twice or choose Quit when you finish drawing lines.

Shading a Cell or Cell Block

Many spreadsheets contain important subtotals and totals that you'll want to highlight in some way. One of the best

Lesson 13

ways to highlight the contents of any cell is to shade the cell. Quattro Pro offers three shading options: **None** (the default), **B**lack, and **G**rey.

![Screenshot of Quattro Pro spreadsheet showing Placement and Line types dialog]

Line placement options — Line types

Figure 13.2 Select a line placement and line type option.

White-on-Black If you choose **B**lack, Quattro Pro will print white text on a black background. Be sure to choose **G**raphics **P**rinter from the **P**rint **D**estination submenu before printing the spreadsheet.

To add shading to a selected cell or block, perform the following steps:

1. Select the cell or cell block you want to shade.

2. Pull down the **S**tyle menu and select **S**hading. The Shading submenu appears, as shown in Figure 13.3.

82

Adding Lines and Shading to Cells and Blocks

3. Select a shading option: None, Grey, or Black. If you selected only one cell, press Enter or click on [Enter] to confirm the selection. You return to the worksheet, and the selected shading is applied to the cell(s).

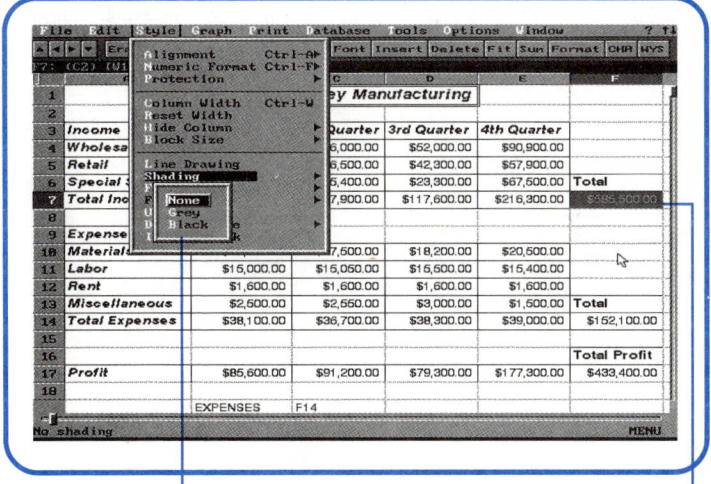

Shading submenu   Cell about to be shaded

Figure 13.3 Select a shading option from the Shading submenu.

In this lesson, you learned how to draw lines around and between cells, and add shading to cells. In the next lesson, you will learn how to apply several style attributes to a cell with a single command.

83

Lesson 14
Formatting Cells with Styles

In this lesson, you'll learn how to specify several formatting options by applying a single style to a selected cell or cell block.

Understanding Styles

In Lessons 12 and 13, you learned how to enhance a spreadsheet by selecting various formatting options for the cells. *Styles* allow you to specify a group of formatting options by applying a single style to a cell or cell block.

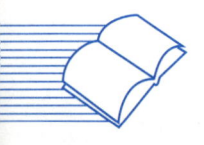

What's a Style? A style is a group of cell formatting options that you can apply to a cell or cell block. If you change the style's definition later, that change affects the formatting of all cells formatted with that style.

Each style contains specifications for one or more of the following options:

Font: Specifies the typeface, point size, text color, and any attributes for text contained in the cell.

Line Drawing: Specifies the line placement and line type options for the cell.

Shading: Adds specified shading to the cell.

Alignment: Specifies general, left, right, or center alignment.

Data Entry: Allows only certain information to be entered in the cell, such as labels only or dates only.

Numeric Format: Specifies the numeric format for the value contained in the cell.

Applying Existing Styles

Quattro Pro comes with several predefined styles, which allow you to add commonly used cell formatting. For example, the HEADING1 style sets the text in 18-point bold type. To use one of these styles, or a style you created, perform the following steps:

1. Select the cell or block you want to format.

2. Open the Style menu and select Use Style, or click on the Style button in the SpeedBar. A list of styles appears, as shown in Figure 14.1.

3. Type the name of the style you want to use and press Enter, or select a style from the list. If you selected only one cell, press Enter or click on [Enter] to confirm the selection. The style is now in effect for the selected cell(s).

Lesson 14

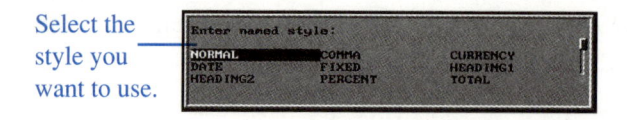

Select the style you want to use.
```
Enter named style:
NORMAL       COMMA        CURRENCY
DATE         FIXED        HEADING1
HEADING2     PERCENT      TOTAL
```

Figure 14.1 Select a style from the list of styles.

> **Panic**
>
> **Formatting Over Styles** When you apply a style to a cell or block, the style formatting options override any cell formatting currently in effect for the selected cells. If you select a formatting option after applying a style, you must choose to clear the style before you can apply the format.

Creating Custom Styles

In addition to Quattro Pro's existing styles, you can create and use your own styles. To create a style, use the following steps:

1. Open the Style menu and select Define Style. The Define Style submenu appears.

2. Select Create. A dialog box appears, prompting you to type a name for the new style.

3. Type a name for the style you want to create and press Enter. The name must differ from any style name currently listed. A dialog box appears, as shown in Figure 14.2.

4. Select the formatting option you want to change and enter your change. When you select a formatting option, a submenu or dialog box appears, prompting you to change the formatting settings.

Formatting Cells with Styles

5. Repeat step 4 until you've changed all the formatting options as desired.

6. Choose **Q**uit and press **Esc** twice to create the style and return to the worksheet screen.

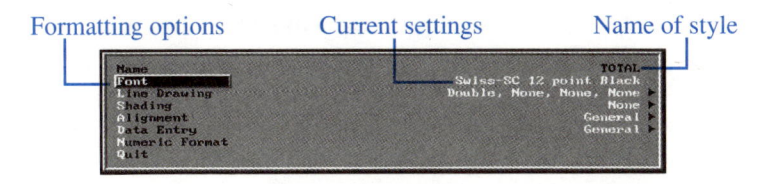

Formatting options   Current settings   Name of style

```
Name                                    TOTAL
Font                        Swiss-SC 12 point Black
Line Drawing                Double, None, None, None
Shading                                    None
Alignment                               General
Data Entry                              General
Numeric Format
Quit
```

Figure 14.2 Use the Define Style dialog box to create a custom style.

Now, when you select **U**se Style from the **S**tyle menu, the style list that appears contains the name of the style you created. You can apply the style by selecting it from the list.

Changing Styles

The most useful aspect of styles is that they allow you to change the formatting options throughout a worksheet simply by changing the options defined by a style.

For example, say you use a style called Total to shade a cell and have its text appear in 16-point Times bold. You have used this style on 12 cells (totals and subtotals) throughout the worksheet. You later decide that you don't want the cells shaded. All you have to do is change the shading option for the style to **N**one. The shading will then be removed from all 12 cells. To change a style, perform the following steps:

Lesson 14

1. Open the Style menu and select Define Style. The Define Style submenu appears.

2. Choose Create. A dialog box appears, prompting you to specify the name of the style you want to change.

3. Type the name of the style you want to change and press Enter, or select the style you want to change from the list. The Define Style dialog box appears (see Figure 14.2).

4. Select the formatting option you want to change and enter your change. When you select a formatting option, a submenu or dialog box appears, prompting you to change the formatting settings.

5. Repeat step 4 until you've changed all the formatting options as desired.

6. Choose Quit and press Esc twice to save your changes and return to the worksheet screen. The new formatting settings are now in effect for all cells to which that style was applied.

In this lesson, you learned how to use styles to apply several formatting settings with a single command. In the next lesson, you'll learn how to set up a page for printing.

Lesson 15

Setting Up a Page for Printing

In this lesson, you will learn how to set page margins and add headers and footers for printing your spreadsheet.

Setting Up a Page

Before you print your spreadsheet, you should check Quattro Pro's page settings to make sure the default settings are appropriate for the spreadsheet you want to print. To display the settings, open the **Print** menu and select **Layout**. The Print Layout Options dialog box appears, as shown in Figure 15.1.

This dialog box allows you to print a header and/or footer on each page, set the page length and margins, select an orientation, and scale the spreadsheet.

Too Wide? If your worksheet is wider than the page, Quattro Pro will move any columns that won't fit on the page to the next page. You can correct the problem in various ways, as explained in this lesson.

89

Lesson 15

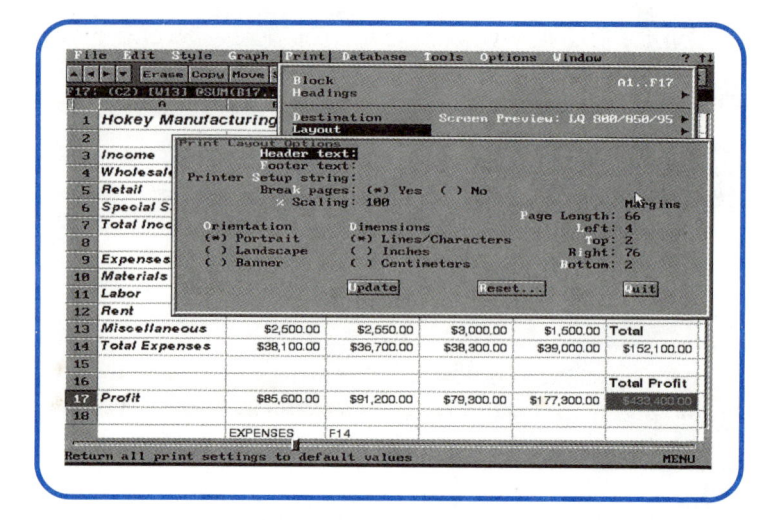

Figure 15.1 Use the Print Layout Options dialog box to change the print settings.

Adding a Header and Footer

A *header* is any text that appears at the top of every page. It can include the name of the spreadsheet, the date, page numbers, or any other text. A *footer* is any text that appears at the bottom of every page. The following codes let you add special elements to the header or footer:

#	Inserts a page number code that inserts the correct page number on each page.
@	Inserts the date.
|	Centers the text.
||	Right-justifies the text.

90

Setting Up a Page for Printing

Figure 15.2 shows sample header and footer entries. To add a header or footer, use the following steps:

1. Open the **Print** menu and select **Layout**.

2. Select **Header Text**, type the header text, and press **Enter**.

3. Select **Footer Text**, type the footer text, and press **Enter**.

4. Select **Quit** to return to the **Print** menu.

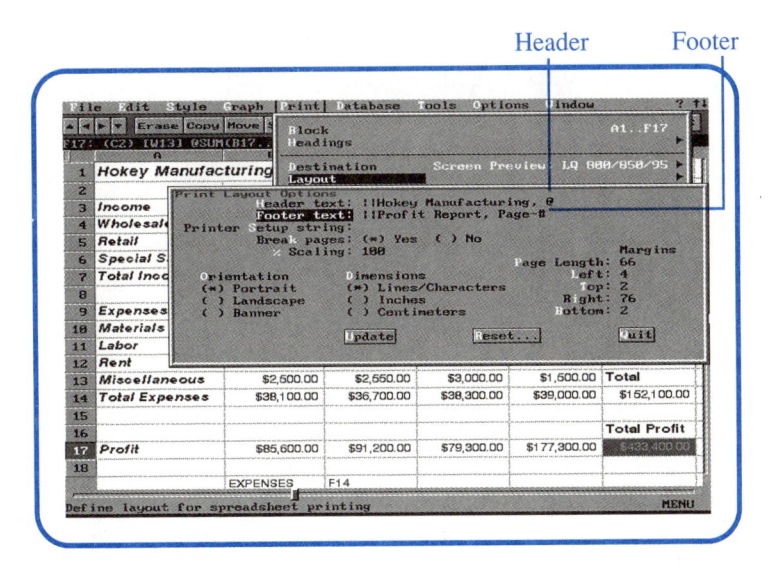

Figure 15.2 Type a header and/or footer to have it print on your spreadsheet.

91

Lesson 15

Setting the Page Length and Margins

By default, Quattro Pro prints a page 66 lines long using one-half inch margins all around. The header and footer are printed inside the margin space. To change the page length and/or margins, use the following steps:

1. Open the Print menu and select Layout. The Print Layout Options dialog box appears.

2. To change the page length, choose Page Length and type the number of lines long you want the page to be. (Dot-matrix printers typically print 66 lines per page. Laser printers typically print 60 lines per page.)

> **Units of Measure** By default, Quattro Pro measures page length in lines per page and margins in characters. To use inches or centimeters instead, choose Dimensions in the dialog box and then choose Inches or Centimeters.

3. Select Top, Left, Right, or Bottom, and type the margin setting you want to use. (The Right margin setting is measured from the left edge of the page. For example, if the setting is 76 characters, the characters are measured from the left edge of the page, leaving approximately one-half inch for the right margin.)

4. Choose Quit to return to the Print menu.

Setting Up a Page for Printing

Selecting a Paper Orientation

By default, Quattro Pro assumes you want to print your spreadsheet on 8.5-by-11-inch paper in portrait orientation. If you have a printer that can print graphics, you can change the orientation setting in the Print Layout Options dialog box.

Orientation If your printer supports graphics, Quattro Pro can rotate text 90 degrees to print each line of text from the top of the page to the bottom (in *landscape orientation*) instead of from left to right across the page (*portrait orientation*). Printing in landscape orientation is useful if you have a wide spreadsheet and are printing on a sheet of paper that is longer than it is wide. If you have a continuous feed printer, you can choose Banner orientation to have a wide spreadsheet printed in landscape orientation over more than one page.

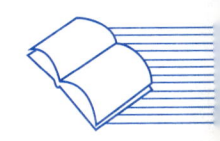

Use the following steps to change the orientation:

1. Open the **Print** menu and select **Layout**.

2. Select **Orientation**. The Orientation options are activated.

3. Select **Portrait**, **Landscape**, or **Banner**.

4. Choose **Quit** to return to the **P**rint menu.

93

Lesson 15

Instant Reset To return the Print Layout settings to the default settings, click on the **Reset** button or press **R** in the Print Layout Options dialog box. Select **All** to reset all the current settings, **Print Block** to reset only the current Print Block setting, **Headings** to reset the Headings entry, or **Layout** to reset all print layout settings.

Automatic Page Breaks

If you print a spreadsheet or part of a spreadsheet that is larger than one page, Quattro Pro automatically breaks pages when necessary. To print the spreadsheet as a continuous block of data (without page breaks and without headers and footers), take the following steps:

1. Open the **Print** menu and select **Layout**.

2. Select **Break Pages** and then select **No**.

3. Choose **Quit** to return to the **Print** menu.

Breaking Pages Manually If Quattro Pro breaks pages at an awkward point, you can add your own page breaks. To break pages, move the selector to the row just below where you want the page to break. Open the **Style** menu and select **Insert Break**. A row is inserted above the cell selector and four dots appear indicating a page break. To remove the page break, delete the row that contains the page break marker.

94

Scaling the Printout

You can enter a scaling percent to increase or reduce the size of the block or spreadsheet you want to print. This changes the size only on the printed copy. You can view the effects of the change using Print Preview, as discussed in the next lesson. To scale the printout, perform the following steps:

1. Open the Print menu and select Layout.

2. Select % Scaling and type a scaling percent. (A percent less than 100% reduces the size of the spreadsheet. A percent greater than 100% increases the size.)

3. Choose Quit to return to the Print menu.

Updating the Print Settings

To save the settings you entered so they will be the default settings for all future worksheet files you will create, select Layout from the Print menu and then select Update. If you don't choose Update, the settings you entered will be saved only for the current worksheet.

In this lesson, you learned how to set up a page for printing. In the next lesson, you will learn how to print your spreadsheet or a selected portion of the spreadsheet.

Lesson 16
Printing a Worksheet

In this lesson, you'll learn how to select a printer and print an entire worksheet or a portion of a worksheet.

Selecting a Printer

When you installed Quattro Pro, you selected a printer to use with the program. You do not have to select this printer each time you use Quattro Pro; it is ready to use. However, at some point you may want to use a different printer. To select a different printer, perform the following steps:

1. Open the Options menu and select Hardware.

2. Select Printers and then select 1st Printer.

3. Select Type of printer. A list of printer brand names appears.

4. Select the brand name of the printer you want to use. If there are several models manufactured by the same company, a submenu appears listing the models.

5. Select the model name of your printer. Many printers have different printing modes. If Quattro Pro displays a Mode submenu, select the desired mode. Quattro Pro returns you to the Type of printer submenu.

Printing a Worksheet

6. If the printer you want to use requires additional settings, select them from this menu.

7. Select Quit three times.

Selecting Print Options

Quattro Pro offers multiple options for printing. To access the print options, open the Print menu, as shown in Figure 16.1. The Print menu contains the following options:

Block: The Block option tells Quattro Pro which block of cells to print. Initially, no block is specified.

Headings: You can select Left Heading to have a range of row headings appear on every page or select Top Heading to have a range of column headings appear on every page.

Repeated Headings   If you print column or row headings, make sure the cells that contain these headings are not in the selected print area (defined by the Block option). If they are, Quattro Pro will print the headings twice.

Destination: The Destination option lets you print the spreadsheet to a Printer, a File, a Binary File, a Graphics Printer, or to Screen Preview.

Graphics Printer   If you used special graphics effects, such as fonts or shading, or if you are printing in Landscape or Banner orientation, choose Graphics Printer. Otherwise, these special effects will not appear on your printout.

97

Lesson 16

Layout: Displays the Print Layout Options dialog box. For more information, refer back to Lesson 15.

Format: This option lets you print the worksheet As Displayed, or print the cell contents as Cell-Formulas rather than as the results of the formulas.

Copies: To print more than one copy of the same worksheet, choose Copies, type the number of copies you want printed, and press Enter.

Adjust Printer: This option allows you to adjust the printer before you start printing. You can choose to Skip Line, Form Feed the page, or Align the print head with the paper in order to start printing at the proper location.

Spreadsheet Print: Selecting this option starts the printing.

Print-To-Fit: Automatically shrinks the block you select (if needed) so that it prints on a single page. (To use this option, you must first select Destination and Graphics Printer.)

Graph Print: Allows you to print a graph. For more information, refer to Lesson 18.

Print Manager: When you print a worksheet, Quattro Pro allows you to continue working while it is printing. Selecting Print Manager displays a screen you can use to control the print operation.

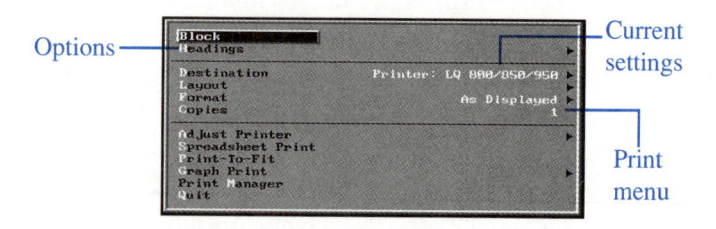

Figure 16.1 The Print pull-down menu.

Printing a Worksheet

Seeing Your Worksheet in Print Preview Mode

Before you print your spreadsheet, you should preview it to determine if it will print correctly. To preview the printout, use the following steps:

1. Open the Print menu and select Block.

2. Move the selection cursor to the cell in the upper left corner of the block you want to print.

3. Type . (period), use the arrow keys to extend the selection over the cells you want to print, and press Enter. Or use your mouse to select the cells and click on [Enter].

4. Select Destination and then select Screen Preview. You return to the Print menu.

5. Select Spreadsheet Print. Quattro Pro displays the current page as it will appear in print, as shown in Figure 16.2.

Exiting Print Preview You can exit Print Preview and return to the worksheet screen at any time by pressing Esc.

While in Print Preview, you can zoom in on an area of the spreadsheet. To zoom in, perform the following steps:

1. Press the plus sign key (+) or select Zoom[+] in the command bar at the top of the screen. A miniature page (called a *guide*) appears in the upper right corner of the screen, as shown in Figure 16.3.

99

Lesson 16

2. Use the arrow keys to select the area of the spreadsheet you want to zoom in on (or use the mouse to drag the selection box in the guide).

3. Press Enter. To zoom out, press the minus sign key (−) or select Unzoom[−].

Full page displayed in Print Preview — Command bar

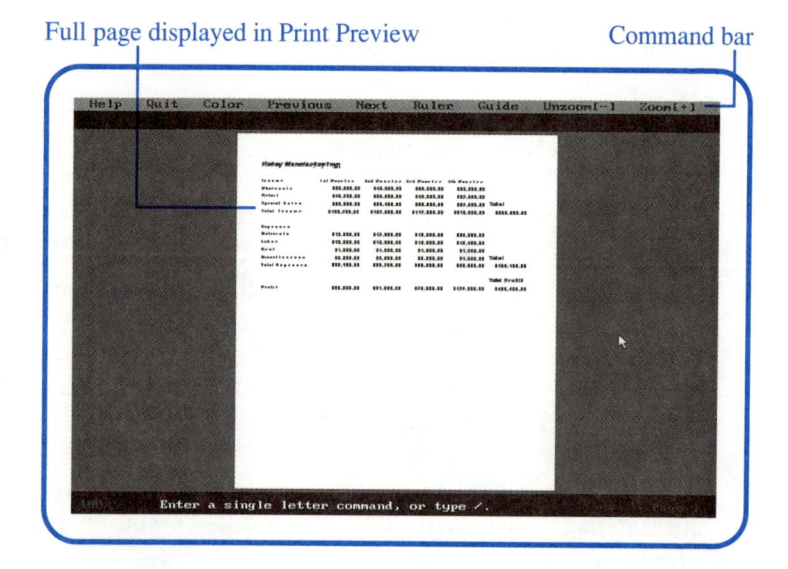

Figure 16.2 A worksheet displayed in Print Preview.

The command bar at the top of the Print Preview screen contains the following commands for controlling Print Preview. To select a command, press the highlighted letter in the command's name or click on the command with your mouse.

100

Printing a Worksheet

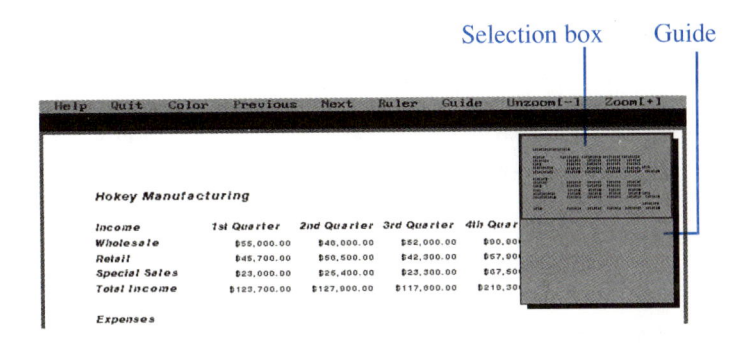

Figure 16.3 When you choose to zoom in on the worksheet, the guide appears in the upper right corner of the screen.

Help displays a help window that describes how to use Print Preview.

Quit cancels Print Preview and returns you to the normal worksheet screen.

Color toggles between black-and-white and color screen displays.

Previous displays the previous page, if there is one.

Next displays the next page, if there is one.

Ruler displays a one-inch grid that overlays the worksheet. This gives you a general idea of the worksheet's layout.

Guide turns the guide in the upper right corner of the screen on or off. This feature is useful if the guide is covering an area of the worksheet you want to view.

101

Unzoom[–] displays a full-page view of the spreadsheet.

Zoom[+] enlarges the view of the spreadsheet by 100%, 200%, or 400%.

Printing a Hard Copy of Your Worksheet

Quattro Pro offers several options for printing a hard copy of your worksheet, as outlined at the beginning of this lesson. To print a worksheet, use the following steps:

1. Open the Print menu.

2. If you have not yet specified a block to print, select Block, move the selector to the upper left cell in the print block, press . (period), use the arrow keys to extend the selection, and press Enter. Or use the mouse to select the cells and click on [Enter].

3. Select Destination. If you are using any special fonts, if Print Orientation is Landscape or Banner, or if you are using Percent Scaling or Print-To-Fit, you must select the Graphics Printer option. Otherwise, select Printer.

4. Set any of the other print options as discussed earlier.

5. Select Spreadsheet Print. Quattro Pro prints your worksheet.

In this lesson, you learned how to set up a printer, set the print options, use Print Preview, and print your worksheet. In the next lesson, you will begin to learn about creating graphs.

Lesson 17
Creating Graphs

In this lesson, you will learn how to use your spreadsheet data to create graphs and place them in your spreadsheets.

Quattro Pro Graphs

With Quattro Pro, you can create 11 types of two-dimensional graphs and four types of three-dimensional graphs. The graph type you choose will depend on your data and on how you want to present that data. For example, a line graph is useful for displaying the relationship of values over time, whereas a bar graph is useful for comparing values at one point in time. Experiment with the graph types to find the best representation of your worksheet. To choose a graph type, perform the following steps:

1. Open the Graph menu and select Graph Type. In WYSIWYG mode, Quattro Pro displays the graph types shown in Figure 17.1. In character mode, the Graph Type submenu appears, displaying a list of graph types.

2. Click on the graph type you want, or use the arrow keys to highlight it and press Enter.

Lesson 17

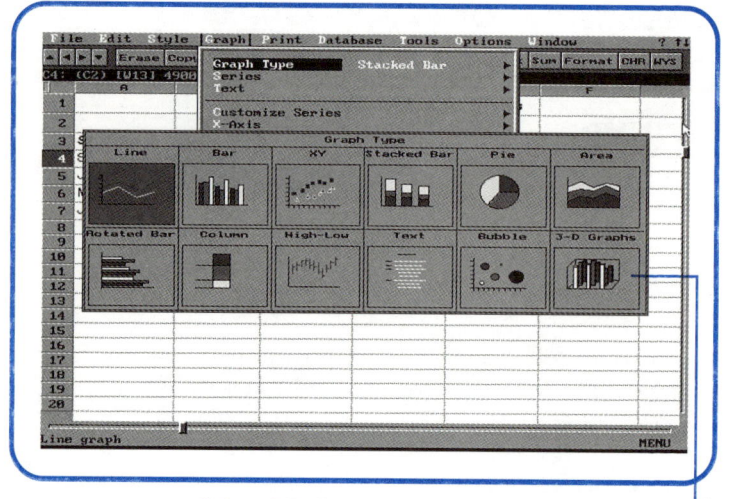

Select 3-D Graphs to view four additional choices.

Figure 17.1 Quattro Pro's graph types.

Selecting the Cells To Graph

To create a graph, you must select the cells that contain the values you want to graph. This is called selecting the *data series*. You can plot up to six different series of values in a single graph. You can also plot an X-axis series to have labels appear below the X-axis (the horizontal axis).

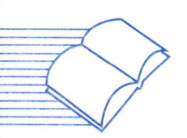

> **Data Series** Each value in a spreadsheet will represent a *data point* on the graph. Several such points comprise a data series. When you are told to select a data series, you must specify a block of cells that contain the data you want to graph.

To select a series to graph, follow these steps:

104

Creating Graphs

1. Open the Graph menu and select Series. The Series submenu appears, as shown in Figure 17.2.

2. Select 1st Series. Quattro Pro takes you back into the worksheet to specify the data for the first series.

3. Move the selector to the first cell containing a value you want to plot, press . (period) and use the arrow keys to extend the selection. Or use the mouse to select the cells. A selected series is shown in Figure 17.3.

4. Press Enter or click on [Enter]. Quattro Pro returns you to the Series submenu. If you want to plot more than one series, repeat steps 2-4 for each series.

5. To have a series of labels appear below the X-axis, select X-Axis Series, select the series of labels you want to use, and then press Enter or click on [Enter].

Series submenu — Ranges for each series

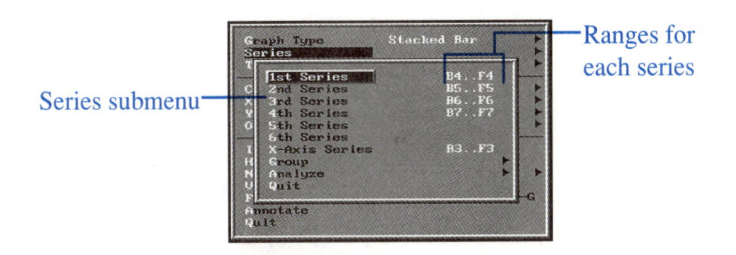

Figure 17.2 The Series submenu.

Fast Graph To create a basic graph in a hurry, select Fast Graph from the Graph menu (or press Ctrl-Gx), select ALL the cells you want to appear in the graph, including any cells you want displayed as labels, and press Enter or click on [Enter].

105

Lesson 17

	A	B	C	D	E	F
1				1992 Regional Sales		
2						
3	Salesperson	1st Qtr	2nd Qtr	3rd Qtr	4th Qtr	Average
4	Susan Q.	$55,000.00	$49,000.00	$51,500.00	$59,000.00	$53,625.00
5	Jack S.	$46,000.00	$48,000.00	$47,000.00	$48,500.00	$47,375.00
6	Marilyn V.	$67,000.00	$57,000.00	$62,500.00	$63,000.00	$62,375.00
7	John B.	$35,000.00	$40,000.00	$52,000.00	$40,500.00	$41,875.00

Figure 17.3 To graph data, you must select a series to graph.

Viewing Your Graph

To view the graph you created, open the Graph menu and select View or press F10. The graph appears on-screen. To display the Zoom and Pan palette for the graph, as shown in Figure 17.4, press both mouse buttons at the same time.

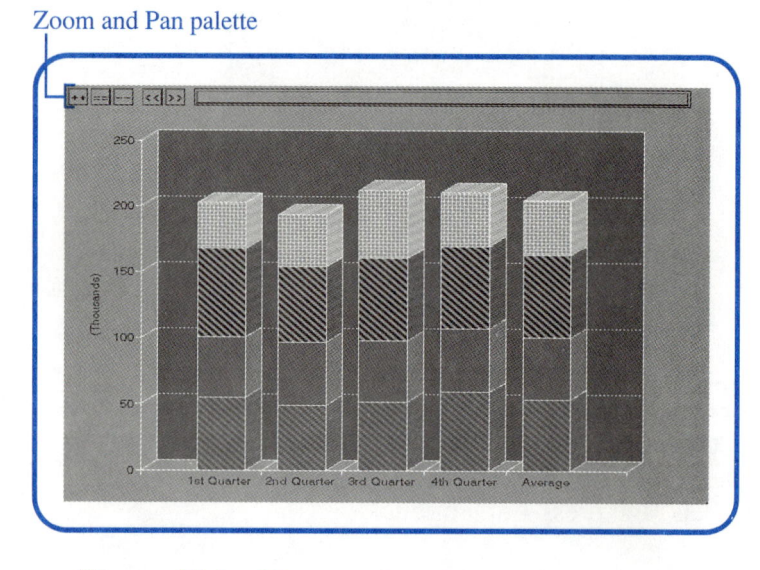

Figure 17.4 You can view the graph you just created.

Creating Graphs

You can click on the following buttons to zoom in on your graph to view portions of the graph in greater detail:

++   Click on ++ to zoom in on the graph. Each time you click on this button, Quattro Pro enlarges the display of a smaller portion of the graph.

--   Click on -- to zoom out and display more of the graph in less detail.

==   Click on == to view the graph in its original size.

\>\>   If you zoom in on a portion of the graph and some of the graph is pushed off-screen, click on >> to view the portion of the graph that is off-screen (called *panning*).

<<   Click on << to pan left.

To turn off the Zoom and Pan palette and continue viewing the graph, click the right mouse button. To return to the worksheet, press Esc or click the right mouse button.

Overlapping Labels?   If the X-axis labels overlap, you can change to a smaller font. Choose Text from the Graph menu and then select Font, Data & Tick Labels, and Point Size. Select a smaller point size from the list.

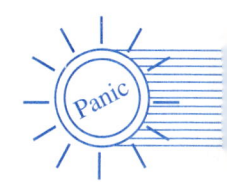

Adding Graph Titles and Legends

You can add a two-line title to the top of the graph, and you can add legends to help explain the data in the graph.

107

Lesson 17

Figure 17.5 shows a bar graph with titles and a legend added. To add a title to a graph, perform the following steps:

1. Open the **G**raph menu and select **T**ext. The Text submenu appears.

2. Select **1**st Line, type the text of the first line of the title, and press Enter.

3. If you want a second line, select **2**nd Line, type a second line of text, and press Enter.

4. Press F10 to see the graph with your changes and press Esc to return to the **G**raph menu.

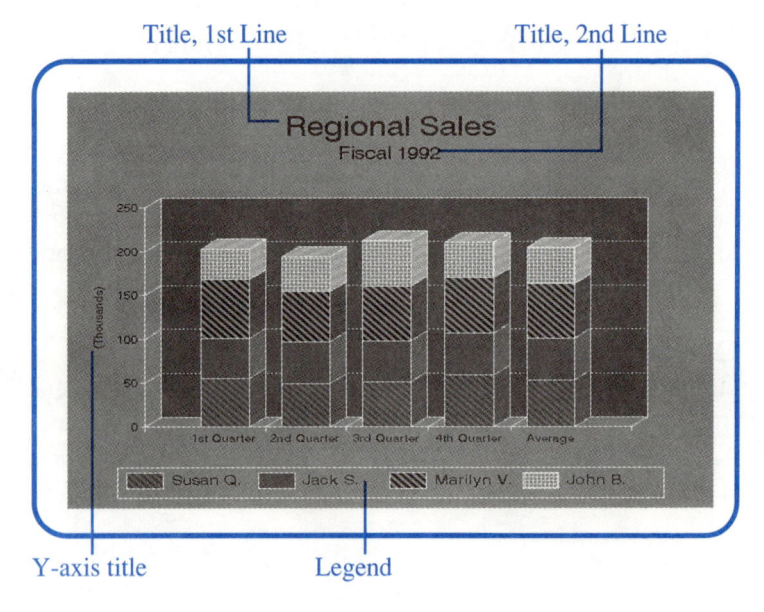

Figure 17.5 A bar graph with titles and legend added.

Adding an X-Axis and Y-Axis Title The Text submenu also contains options for entering an X-Title and a Y-Title.

A graph legend helps clarify the meaning of the colors, markers, or patterns in the graph. To add a legend to a graph, take the following steps:

1. Open the Graph menu and select Text. The Text submenu appears.

2. Select Legends.

3. Select the series for which you want to create a legend.

4. Type the text for the legend or type \ followed by the cell address that contains the text you want to appear in the legend (for example, type \A4).

5. Press Enter.

6. To add a series to the legend, repeat steps 2-5.

7. Press F10 to see the graph with the legend and press Esc to return to the Graph menu.

Saving, Retrieving, and Inserting Graphs

When you save a worksheet, Quattro Pro saves the graph along with the worksheet. If you want to create more than one graph for a worksheet, you must save each graph using a unique name. You can then retrieve the graph(s) or insert the graph(s) in your worksheet later.

Lesson 17

Saving a Graph

Saving a graph under a unique name prevents you from accidentally overwriting the graph later and is necessary if you are going to have more than one graph associated with the worksheet. To save a graph, perform the following steps:

1. Open the Graph menu and select Name. The Name submenu appears.

2. Select Create. The Create dialog box appears.

3. Type a name for the graph (up to 15 characters) and press Enter.

Retrieving a Saved Graph

If there is only one graph associated with your worksheet, the graph is retrieved when the worksheet file is opened. If you have saved more than one graph with a worksheet, you must follow these steps to retrieve it:

1. Open the Graph menu and select Name.

2. Select Display. A list of all the graphs stored is displayed.

3. Select the name of the graph you want to see. The graph appears on-screen.

Inserting a Graph into a Worksheet

You can insert a graph into your worksheet to have the graph appear side-by-side with the data it is clarifying. (You can insert more than one graph into a worksheet.) To insert a graph, perform the following steps:

1. Open the Graph menu and select Insert. Quattro Pro displays a dialog box, prompting you to select the graph you want to insert.

2. Select the name of the graph you want to insert.

3. Select the cell block into which you want the graph inserted. Quattro Pro will automatically size the graph to fit into the selected cell block.

4. Press Enter. Quattro Pro inserts the graph in the specified location.

In this lesson, you learned how to create, save, retrieve, and insert graphs. In the next lesson, you will learn how to enhance these basic graphs and print them.

Lesson 18
Enhancing and Printing Graphs

In this lesson, you will learn how to enhance, annotate, and print your graphs.

Enhancing Your Graph

You can enhance virtually every aspect of a Quattro Pro graph by using the four options in the **G**raph menu: **C**ustomize Series, **X**-Axis, **Y**-Axis, and **O**verall.

The following sections explain these options in greater detail.

Customizing a Series

Each data series on a graph has a unique color and fill pattern that helps distinguish it from the other series on the graph. You can change the color and fill pattern by performing the following steps:

1. Open the Graph menu and select Customize Series. The Graph Customize dialog box appears (see Figure 18.1).

2. Select Series and select the number of the series you want to modify.

Enhancing and Printing Graphs

3. Select Color and select a color for the series.

4. Select Fill Pattern and select a fill pattern for the series.

5. If you have a bar graph, you can select Bar width and enter a percent to increase or decrease the bar width.

6. To insert a label that will appear within the graph above the data for this series, select Interior Label Block and type a label.

7. To make the current settings the default settings, choose Update. To reset the settings, choose Reset. To apply the settings only to the current graph, choose Quit.

Select the series you want to specify.

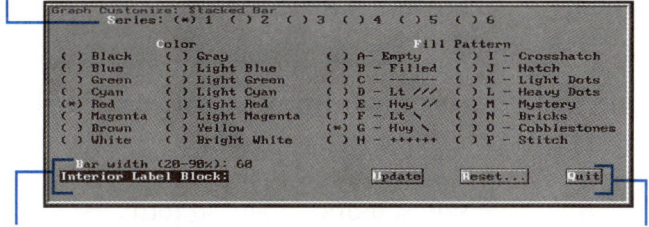

These options may not appear for some graph types.

Options may differ depending on graph type.

Figure 18.1 The Graph Customize dialog box lets you change the color and fill pattern for a series.

Customizing the X- and Y-Axes

If you select the X-Axis or Y-Axis from the Graph menu, a dialog box appears like the one in Figure 18.2, offering the following options:

Lesson 18

Scale | Select Automatic or Manual; if you select Manual, you need to enter Low, High, and Increment settings.

Low | Enter the minimum value that you want plotted.

High | Enter the maximum value you want plotted.

Increment | Specify the number of divisions for the axis.

Format of Ticks | Select the type of value and the display mode for the tick marks on the axis.

No. of Minor Ticks | If the axis labels are too crowded, you can use this option to delete some of the tick marks.

Display Scaling | Quattro Pro automatically scales each axis to fit the series assigned to it and adds the definition of the numbers in thousands, millions, and so forth.

Mode | Values can be scaled in Normal or Logarithmic mode.

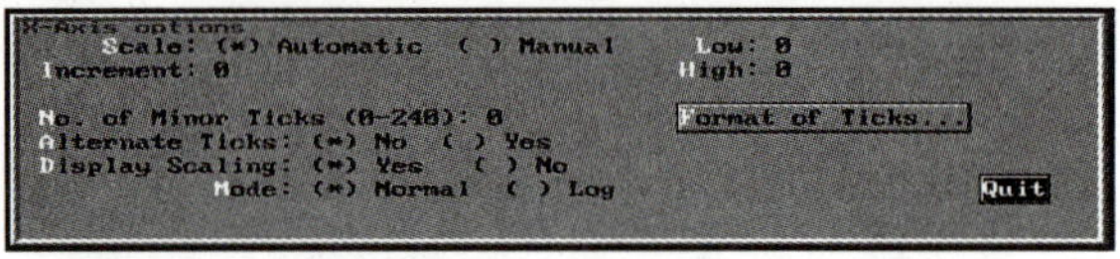

```
X-Axis options
    Scale: (*) Automatic  ( ) Manual       Low: 0
Increment: 0                                High: 0
No. of Minor Ticks (0-248): 0              Format of Ticks...
Alternate Ticks: (*) No  ( ) Yes
Display Scaling: (*) Yes  ( ) No
          Mode: (*) Normal  ( ) Log                    Quit
```

Figure 18.2 Use the Options dialog box to change the format settings for the X- or Y-axis. (X-axis options are shown here.)

Enhancing and Printing Graphs

To modify either axis, use the following steps:

1. Open the Graph menu and select X-Axis or Y-Axis. If you select the X-Axis, the X-axis submenu appears (see Figure 18.2); the Y-axis submenu looks similar.

2. Change any of the settings, as explained earlier.

3. Choose Quit.

Changing the Overall Formatting for Your Graph

If you select Overall from the Graph menu, Quattro Pro displays the Graph Overall dialog box, as shown in Figure 18.3. This dialog box contains the following options for controlling the overall appearance of your graph:

Outlines	Allows you to add enhancements such as boxes and drop shadows to Titles, to the Legend, or to the entire Graph.
Colors	Allows you to set the colors for the Grid, the Fill pattern, and the Background.
Grid Line Style	Lets you choose the type of line used for the grid.
Grid	Lets you choose to display a Horizontal grid, a Vertical grid, or Both horizontal and vertical, or Clear the grid.
Use Colors	Allows you to use colors in the graph or turn off colors to have the graph appear in black-and-white.

Lesson 18

Add Depth — Lets you view the graph in 3-D view (when set to **Y**es) or turn off 3-D view (when set to **N**o).

Drop Shadow Colors — Lets you select the colors used for creating drop shadows.

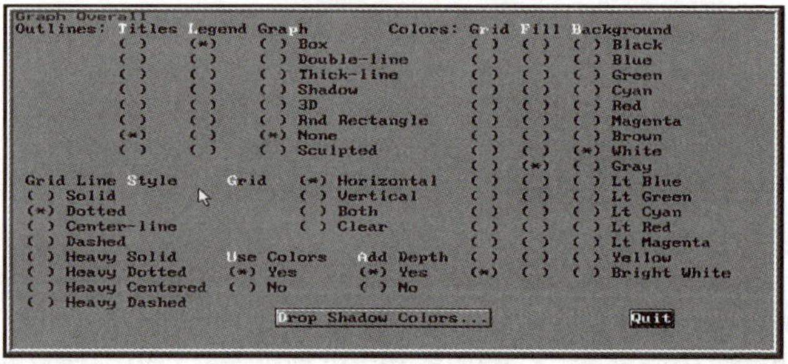

Figure 18.3 Use the Graph Overall dialog box to control the overall appearance of the graph.

Annotating Your Graph

The *Graph Annotator* is a built-in graphics editor that you can use to draw lines, arrows, text boxes, circles, and other graphic elements on your graph. To access the Graph Annotator, open the Graph menu and select Annotator. Your graph appears in the Annotator, as shown in Figure 18.4.

116

Enhancing and Printing Graphs

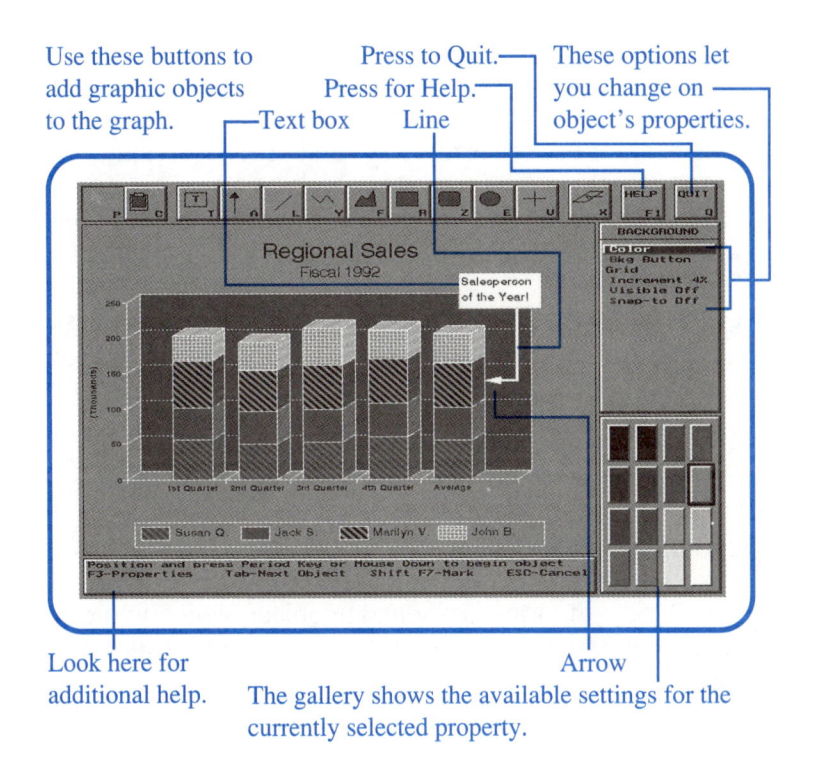

Use these buttons to add graphic objects to the graph.

Press to Quit.
Press for Help.
Text box   Line

These options let you change on object's properties.

Look here for additional help.

Arrow

The gallery shows the available settings for the currently selected property.

Figure 18.4 A graph displayed in the Annotator. A text box has been added.

Adding a Graphics Object to the Graph

The toolbox at the top of the Annotator allows you to add objects to your graph. For example, to add a text box to your graph, perform the following steps:

117

Lesson 18

1. Click on the T button or press /T.

2. Click the mouse pointer where you want the text box to appear, or use the arrow keys and press . (period).

3. Start typing the text you want to appear in the text box. To start a new line in the text box, press Ctrl-Enter.

4. To change the color of the text or the background, press F3 and use the properties and gallery on the right side of the Annotator to set the color and any other properties, such as alignment.

Selecting Objects

Each object you draw is a separate object, which you can delete or modify. To select an object, use the following steps:

1. Click on the P button on the left end of the toolbox or press /P.

2. Click on the object you want to select or press the Tab key to cycle through the various objects.

Small rectangles appear around the selected object to show that it is selected (see Figure 18.5). Once an object is selected, you can perform any of several operations on the object:

- To delete a selected object, press the Del key.

- To move a selected object, drag it with the mouse or use the arrow keys.

Enhancing and Printing Graphs

- To increase or reduce the size of an object, move the mouse pointer over one of the object's handles, hold down the mouse button, and drag the handle.

- To change the color of an object or any of its properties, press F3 and use the palette on the right side of the Annotator to change the properties.

Handles

Figure 18.5 When you select an object, handles appear around it.

Printing a Graph

Follow these steps to print the current graph (if you want to print a different graph you named and saved, retrieve the saved graph before performing the following steps):

1. Open the Print menu and select Graph Print.

2. Select Destination.

3. Select Graph Printer.

4. If you want to print the current graph (the one you see if you press F10), select Go. If you want to print a different graph, select Name, select the name of the graph you want to print, and then press Enter. Now select Go.

119

Lesson 19

Creating a Simple Database

In this lesson, you'll learn how to create and save a database.

Database Basics

A *database* is a tool used for storing, organizing, and retrieving information. For example, if you want to save the names and addresses of all the people on your holiday card list, you could create a database for storing the following information for each person: first name, last name, street number, and so on. Each piece of information is entered into a separate *field*. All of the fields for each person on the list make up a *record*. In Quattro Pro, a cell is a field, and a row of field entries makes a record. Figure 19.1 shows a database and its component parts.

You must observe the following rules when you enter information into your database:

- *Field Names:* You must enter field names in the first row of the database; for example, type **FNAME** for first name and **LNAME** for the last name. The field names can be no longer than 15 characters and cannot contain any of the following operators: +, –, *, /, or ^. A field name cannot be in use elsewhere on the worksheet, as a block name or as a field entry. Do NOT skip a row between the field names row and the first record.

Creating a Simple Database

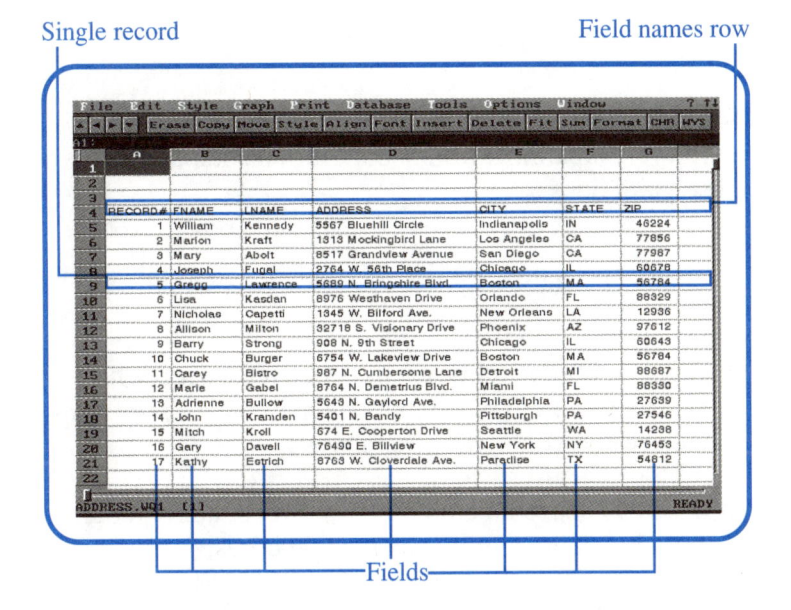

Figure 19.1 The component parts of a database.

- *Records:* Each record must be in a separate row, with no empty rows between records. The cells in a given column must contain information of the same type. For example, if you have a ZIP CODE column, all cells in that column must contain a ZIP code. You can create a calculated field; one that uses information from another field of the same record and produces a result. (To do so, enter a formula, as explained in Lesson 5.)

Record Numbering Adding a column that numbers the records is a good idea. If the records are sorted incorrectly, you can use the numbered coumn to restore the records to their original order.

121

Lesson 19

Creating a Database

To create a database, enter data into the cells as you would if you were creating a worksheet. As you enter data, follow these guidelines:

- You must enter field names in the top row of the database.

- Type field entries into each cell to create a record. (You can leave a field blank, but you may run into problems later when you sort the database.)

- Do NOT leave an empty row between the field names and the records, or between any records.

- If you want to enter street numbers with the street names, start the entry with an apostrophe so that Quattro Pro interprets the entry as text instead of as a value.

Once you've entered your records, you can transform the worksheet into a database using the following steps:

1. Open the Database menu and select Query.

2. Select Block. Quattro Pro prompts you to select the block of cells you want included in the database.

3. Select the block of cells that comprise the database, including the row with the field names, and press Enter or click on [Enter].

4. Select Assign Names. Quattro Pro assigns block names to each column using the field names in the top row as the block names.

5. Select Quit to return to the worksheet.

Creating a Simple Database

Additional Records Repeat these steps whenever you add records to your database in order to update the database definition.

Adding Records

To add records to the database, enter each new record in the bottom row of the database. Remember to repeat the steps in the preceding section to redefine the database; otherwise, the new records will not be included in the database.

Adding Columns

If you add more columns of information, you are adding additional fields. Remember to redefine the database block after adding the columns.

Saving the Database

After you've entered data and named the database cell block, save the database as you would save any worksheet. It is a good idea to save database files in a separate directory. (For more information on working with directories, see Lesson 21.)

Lesson 20

Sorting, Searching, and Printing a Database

In this lesson, you will learn how to sort a database, locate specific records, and print a database or a portion of it.

Sorting a Database

You can enter records in your database in any order. You can then use the Sort feature to sort the records in various ways. For example, you can sort the records numerically in ascending order by ZIP code or alphabetically in descending order by Last Name.

The sorting instructions you give Quattro Pro are referred to as *sort keys*. The sort key tells Quattro Pro which column to sort on and whether to sort in *ascending order* (1,2,3... or A,B,C...) or *descending order* (10,9,8... or Z,Y,X...). You can use more than one sort key to sort your records. For example, you can sort records first by ZIP code and then by Last Name. Quattro Pro would sort the records numerically by ZIP code; any records having the same ZIP code entry would then be sorted by last name.

Sorting, Searching, and Printing a Database

Common Sorting Error When you sort a database, do not include the top row—the one with the field names—in the block of cells to sort. If you do, it will be sorted along with the other rows and may end up not being the top row.

To sort a database, perform the following steps:

1. Open the Database menu and select Sort. The Sort submenu appears, as shown in Figure 20.1.

2. Select Block. Quattro Pro takes you back to the worksheet.

3. Move the selector to the upper left cell in the block that you want to sort. (Don't include the field names!)

4. Press . (period) to anchor the selector and use the arrow keys to extend the selection over the entire block of cells. Or drag the mouse over the desired cells.

Named Block If you've named the block, you can type the name of the block to select it.

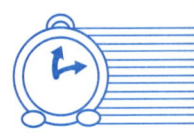

5. Press Enter or click on [Enter]. You return to the Sort submenu.

6. Select 1st Key. Quattro Pro returns you to the worksheet.

7. Move the selector to the column that you want to sort the records by, or type in the name of the column from the field names row, and press Enter or click on [Enter]. Quattro Pro displays the Sort Order dialog box.

125

Lesson 20

8. Type **D** to sort in descending order or **A** to sort in ascending order, and press Enter or click on the Enter button.

9. To enter another sort key, repeat steps 6-8 for the 2nd Key.

10. Select **Go**. Quattro Pro sorts the records accordingly. Figure 20.2 shows the original records sorted in ascending order by last name.

Sort Submenu

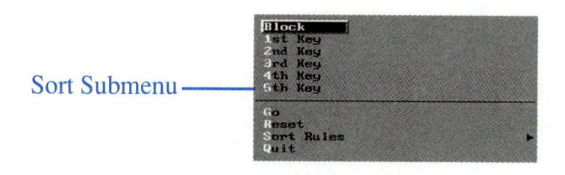

Figure 20.1 The Sort submenu lets you select the block you want to sort and enter sort keys.

Records sorted in ascending order by last name

Figure 20.2 Records sorted in ascending order by last name.

Modifying the Sort Rules

With some databases, the standard rules for sorting are not useful. For example, if the field column you selected as the

126

Sorting, Searching, and Printing a Database

1st sort key has both label and value entries, Quattro Pro automatically places the records with values at the bottom of the database. To change the sort rules, open the Database menu, select Sort, and select Sort Rules. The Sort Rules submenu appears, offering the following options:

Numbers Before Labels: Select Yes if you want records that contain numbers to be positioned at the top of the list.

Sort Rows/Columns: If your database is set up so that each record is entered in a column instead of a row, use this option to sort on columns.

Label Order: Select Dictionary if you want the labels in the column to sort Aa Bb. ASCII order sorts all uppercase letters first, ABC and so forth.

Change the sort rules as desired and then choose Quit.

Searching for Records

You can have Quattro Pro search for specific records in your database. To search for records, you must perform the following three steps:

1. Define the block of records you want to search.

2. Create a search criteria table to tell Quattro Pro what to look for.

3. Select Database/Query/Locate.

Defining the Records To Search

Before you can search a database, you must tell Quattro Pro which records to search through. To define a block of records, perform the following steps:

127

Lesson 20

1. Open the Database menu and select Query. The Query submenu opens.

2. Select Block option. Quattro Pro returns you to the worksheet.

3. Move the selector to the upper left cell in the block that you want to search. (Be sure to include the field names!)

> **Include Field Names?** Unlike the Sort operation, the Search operation requires you to include field names in the cell block. Quattro Pro uses the field names during its search.

4. Press . (period) to anchor the selector and use the arrow keys to extend the selection over the entire block of cells. Or drag the mouse over the desired cells.

5. Press Enter. You return to the Query submenu.

Creating a Search Criteria Table

The search criteria table tells Quattro Pro what to look for. As shown in Figure 20.3, the table consists of a row that is identical to the field names row and an empty row that allows you to specify what to look for. In Figure 20.3, the criteria table is telling Quattro Pro to find all records that have the entry Burger in the LNAME field. To create a search criteria table, perform the following steps:

1. Copy the field names from the top row of the database to a blank row below the last record. Leave two blank rows between the last record and this row.

2. Enter the label CRITERIA in the row above the copied row, to indicate the purpose of this table.

Sorting, Searching, and Printing a Database

3. Open the Database menu, select Query, and select Criteria Table.

4. Select the cells that make up the criteria table and press Enter or click on [Enter]. The cells include the row with the field names and the row just below it (in Figure 20.3, this would be A24..G25).

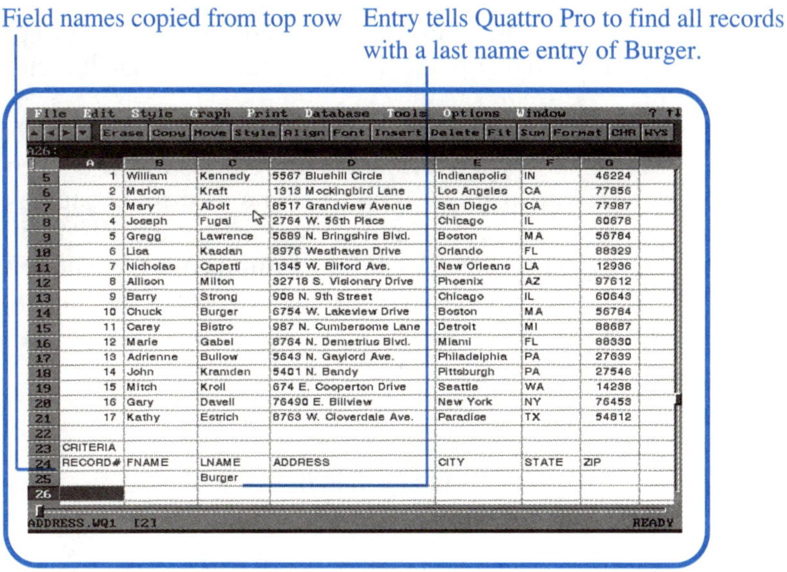

Field names copied from top row   Entry tells Quattro Pro to find all records with a last name entry of Burger.

Figure 20.3   The search criteria table lets you tell Quattro Pro what to look for.

Locating Records

Once you've defined the block you want to search and created a search criteria table, you are ready to tell Quattro Pro what to look for. To do this, you must type an entry in the field in which you want to search. This entry can include the following:

129

Text: Type an entry to find an exact match. For example, if you are searching for a record with a last name entry of Burger, you can type `Burger` in the LNAME field of the search criteria table.

Wild-card entries: Wild cards allow you to perform a more general search. Type `?` in place of a single character, `*` in place of a group of characters, or `~` to find an entry that does not match the characters you type. For example, Sm?th will find Smith, Smoth, and Smeth. Sm* will find Smith, Smythe, and Smegle. ~Burger will find all records with a last name entry that does not match *Burger*.

Formulas: Type a formula to find entries within a given range. For example, you can type a formula such as `(ZIP>46000)` to find all records that have a ZIP code entry greater than 46000. The formula must be entered within parentheses and must include one of the following operators:

=	equal to
>	greater than
>=	greater than or equal to
<	less than
<=	less than or equal to
< >	not equal to

To locate records, perform the following steps:

1. Move the selector in the search criteria table to the cell directly beneath the field name that you want to use in the query. For example, if you want to find a record by the Last Name entry, move the selector to the cell under the LNAME field in the search criteria table.

2. Type an entry to specify what you want to search for. For example, type `Burger` as in Figure 20.3.

3. Open the Database menu and select Query.

4. Select Locate. The selection cursor moves to the first record that meets the criteria. Press ↓ to move to the next record that matches the search criteria.

Extracting Records

You can use the Query option to have Quattro Pro find all the records that match the specified criteria and copy the records to a separate block of cells. (The records remaining in their original location are copied to a separate table.) To extract the records in this way, perform the following steps:

1. Copy the field names from the top row of the database to a blank row below the search criteria table. Leave two blank rows between the criteria table and this row, as shown in Figure 20.4.

2. Enter the label OUTPUT in the row above the copied row, to indicate the purpose of this table.

3. Open the Database menu, select Query, and select Output Block.

4. Select the cells that contain the field names you copied and press Enter or click on [Enter].

5. Type an entry in the search criteria table to specify the records you want to extract.

6. Select Extract. Quattro Pro copies the located records from the database to the output block.

Field names copied from top row

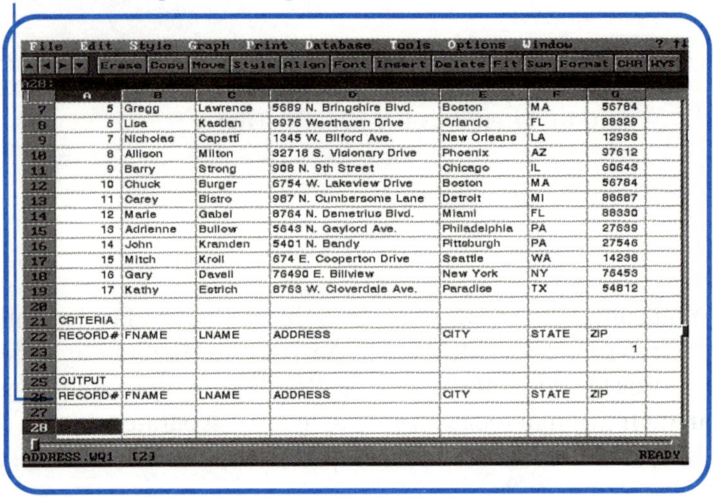

	A	B	C	D	E	F	G
7	5	Gregg	Lawrence	5689 N. Bringshire Blvd.	Boston	MA	56784
8	6	Lisa	Kasdan	8976 Westhaven Drive	Orlando	FL	88329
9	7	Nicholas	Capetti	1345 W. Bilford Ave.	New Orleans	LA	12936
10	8	Allison	Milton	32718 S. Visionary Drive	Phoenix	AZ	97612
11	9	Barry	Strong	908 N. 9th Street	Chicago	IL	60643
12	10	Chuck	Burger	6754 W. Lakeview Drive	Boston	MA	56784
13	11	Carey	Bistro	987 N. Cumbersome Lane	Detroit	MI	88687
14	12	Marie	Gabel	8764 N. Demetrius Blvd.	Miami	FL	88330
15	13	Adrienne	Bullow	5643 N. Gaylord Ave.	Philadelphia	PA	27639
16	14	John	Kramden	5401 N. Bandy	Pittsburgh	PA	27546
17	15	Mitch	Kroll	674 E. Cooperton Drive	Seattle	WA	14238
18	16	Gary	Davell	76490 E. Billview	New York	NY	76453
19	17	Kathy	Estrich	8763 W. Cloverdale Ave.	Paradise	TX	54812
20							
21	CRITERIA						
22	RECORD#	FNAME	LNAME	ADDRESS	CITY	STATE	ZIP
23							1
24							
25	OUTPUT						
26	RECORD#	FNAME	LNAME	ADDRESS	CITY	STATE	ZIP
27							
28							

Figure 20.4 To extract records, you must first define an output block.

Printing a Database Report

Printing a database report is the same as printing a worksheet. To print a database, follow these steps:

1. Open the Print menu.
2. Select Block, select the cell block you want to print, and press Enter or click on [Enter].
3. Select Spreadsheet Print.

Lesson 21
Managing Your Files

In this lesson, you will learn how to manage your worksheet and database files using Quattro Pro's File Manager.

Running the File Manager

Quattro Pro's File Manager simplifies many of the DOS file-related tasks including listing, copying, and deleting files. To open the File Manager, perform the following steps:

1. Open the File menu and select Utilities.

2. Select File Manager. The File Manager window appears, as shown in Figure 21.1.

3. To display the directory tree (as shown on the right side of the figure), open the Tree menu and choose Open.

The File Manager window contains a menu bar and the following three panes: a control pane (which allows you to change drives and directories), a file list pane, and a directory tree pane.

133

Lesson 21

[Figure showing File Manager window with labels: Control pane, File list pane, Pull-down menu bar, Directory tree pane]

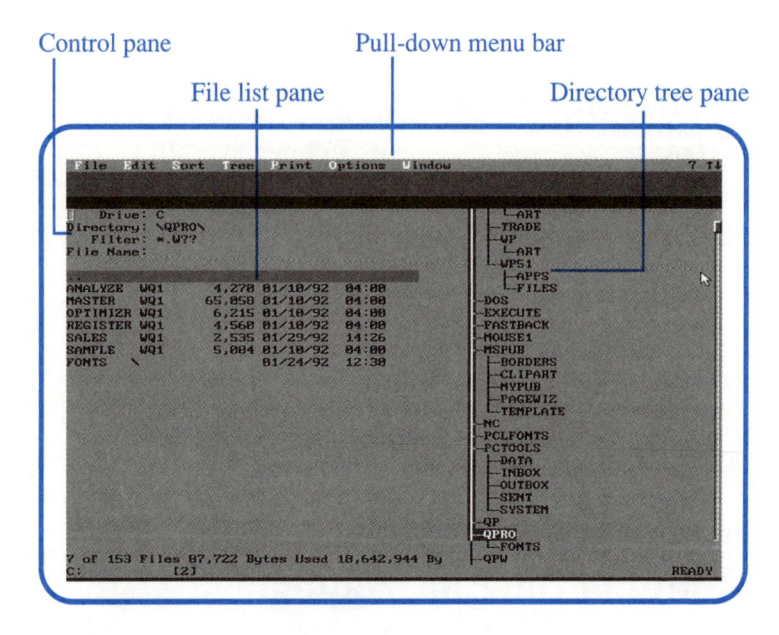

Figure 21.1 The File Manager window.

A Window Is a Window The File Manager is in a separate window, just like a worksheet. You can control the size of the window, or tile or move the window just as you can with any other Quattro Pro window. Simply open the Window menu and select an option.

Using the Control Pane

The control pane lets you change drives and directories, type a wild-card entry to filter the file list, or type a file name. To activate the control pane with your mouse, simply click inside the pane. With the keyboard, use the Tab key to move from pane to pane, and use the arrow keys to move within a pane. Once in the control pane, you can perform the following operations:

134

Managing Your Files

- *Change Drives:* Move the cursor up to the Drive: prompt, type the letter of the drive, and press Enter.

- *Change Directories:* Move the cursor to the Directory: prompt, type a path to the directory, and press Enter. For example, type `\QPRO\DATA\`. The path tells Quattro Pro the location of the files.

- *Filter the File List:* By default, Quattro Pro displays a list of Quattro Pro files only (files with the extension .WQ1). To view a different listing, move the cursor to the Filter: prompt and type a filter entry. For example, you can type `*.*` to view a list of all files in the current directory.

- *Specify a File:* If you know the file you want to work with, you can select it by typing its name next to the File Name: prompt instead of selecting it from the file list.

Using the File List

You can use the file list to select the files you want to copy or to select a subdirectory of the current directory. By default, the files are sorted in alphabetical order. To sort the files differently, perform the following steps:

1. Open the Sort menu.

2. Select a sort order: Name, Timestamp, Extension, Size, or DOS Order.

Parent Directories   The two dots .. at the top of the file list represent the directory that is one directory higher than the current directory. To move up a directory, select the dots.

135

Lesson 21

Using the Directory Tree

The directory tree allows you to move quickly from one directory to another. To activate a directory, simply select it from the tree: either click on it with the mouse, or tab to the tree pane, use the up- and down-arrow keys to highlight the directory, and then press Enter. When you select a directory, the file list changes to show a list of files in that directory.

Making a Directory

It is a good practice to store related files in the same directory to make it easier to find the files. With the File Manager, you can create directories without having to exit to DOS. You can then save files to this directory and/or move files into it as desired. To create a directory, perform the following steps:

1. Change to the drive and directory under which you want the new directory to appear.

2. Open the File menu and select Make Dir.

3. Type a name for the new directory (up to eight characters) and press Enter or click on the Enter button.

Selecting Files

Before you can copy, move, or delete files, you must select the files using one of the following methods:

Managing Your Files

- *Mouse Select:* Click on each file you want to select. You can unselect a selected file by clicking on it again.

- *Keyboard Select:* Highlight the file you want to select and press Shift-F7. You can unselect a file by highlighting it and pressing Shift-F7 again.

- *Menu Select:* Highlight the file you want to select, open the Edit menu, and choose Select File.

- *Select All Files:* To select all the files that are displayed, press Alt-F7 or open the Edit menu and select All Select.

Copying and Moving Files

The File Manager allows you to quickly move or copy files from one directory to another. Perform the following steps:

1. Select the file(s) you want to copy or move.

2. Open the Edit menu and select Move or Copy.

3. Change to the drive or directory where you want the files moved or copied.

4. Open the Edit menu and choose Paste. The files are moved or copied to the specified drive and directory.

Bypass the Edit Menu   To move files, select the files and press Shift-F8. To copy files, select the files and press Shift-F9.

Lesson 21

Erasing Files

Useless files can clutter a disk, so you should delete any files you no longer have need for. To delete files, perform the following steps:

Careful! Quattro Pro does not allow you to undelete files. Make sure you will never again need a file before deleting it.

1. Select the file(s) you want to erase.

2. Open the Edit menu and select Erase. A warning box appears, asking you to confirm the operation.

3. Choose Yes to confirm or No to cancel.

Renaming Files

The **R**ename command allows you to rename and/or move a file. To rename a file, perform the following steps:

1. Highlight the file you want to rename, but do not select it.

2. Open the Edit menu and select Rename, or press F2. A dialog box appears, showing the current location and name of the file.

3. Change the name as desired. If you want to move the file while renaming it, edit the path statement.

4. Press Enter.

Overtime

Appendix A
Table of Functions

As explained in Lesson 6, Quattro Pro includes hundreds of built-in functions that perform complex mathematical operations. For more information and a complete list of functions, refer to the Quattro Pro documentation. The most commonly used functions are described following:

Mathematical Functions

@ABS(*value*)   Calculates the absolute value of a number.

@RAND   Calculates a random number between 0 and 1.

@ROUND(*value,digits*)   Rounds a value to a specified number of digits.

@SQRT(*value*)   Calculates the square root of a value.

Statistical Functions

@AVG(*range*)   Calculates the average of a series of values.

@COUNT(*range*)   Calculates the number of cells in a range that contains numerical values.

Appendix A

@MAX(*range*) — Finds the largest value in a range of numerical values.

@MIN(*range*) — Finds the smallest value in a range of numerical values.

@SUM(*range*) — Calculates the total of the values in range of numerical values.

String Functions

@LOWER(*string*) — Changes the character in string to lowercase.

@PROPER(*string*) — Changes the first letter in each of the words to uppercase.

@REPEAT(*string,num*) — Repeats the string the number of times specified.

@UPPER(*string*) — Changes the characters in the string to uppercase.

Financial Functions

@CTERM(*interest rate, future value,present value*) — Calculates the number of compounding periods needed to grow the present value to a future value.

@DDB(*cost,salvage,life, period*) — Calculates depreciation using the double declining balance method.

@FV(*payments,interest rate, term*) — Calculates the future value of an investment.

@IRR(*guess,block*) — Calculates the internal rate of return.

@NPER(*interest rate,payment, principal*) — Calculates the number of periods needed to reach a target value.

@NPV(*interest rate,block*) — Calculates the net present value of a series of cash flows.

@PAYMT(*interest rate,per, nper,principal*) — Calculates the payment on a loan.

@PV(*interest rate,periods, payment*) — Calculates the present value of an annuity.

@RATE(*future value, present value,term*) — Calculates the interest rate needed to reach a future value.

@SLN(*cost,salvage,life*) — Calculates depreciation using the straight line method.

@SYD(*cost,salvage,life, period*) — Calculates depreciation using the sum of the years' digit method.

@TERM(*payments,interest rate, future value*) — Calculates the number of periods needed to reach a future value.

Date and Time Functions

@DATE(*year,month,day*) — Converts the date into a serial number.

@DAY(*serial date*) — Converts the serial number to a date.

@HOUR(*serial time*) — Converts the serial time to a number.

@MONTH(*serial date*) — Converts the serial date to a number.

@TODAY — Displays the current date.

@YEAR(*serial date*) — Converts the serial date to a number.

Appendix A

Database Statistical Functions

@DAVG(*block,column,criteria*) Averages the entries in a numeric field. The criteria portion of the argument is optional, but if used averages only the records specified by the criteria.

@DCOUNT(*block,column, criteria*) Counts the number of entries in the specified field. The criteria portion of the argument is optional, but if used counts only the records specified by the criteria.

@DMAX(*block,column,criteria*) Finds the largest value in the field. The criteria portion of the argument is optional, but if used searches only the records specified by the criteria for the largest value.

@DMIN(*block,column,criteria*) Finds the smallest value in the field. The criteria portion of the argument is optional, but if used searches only the records specified by the criteria for the smallest value.

@DSTD(*block,column,criteria*) Calculates the standard deviation of the values in the field. The criteria portion of the argument is optional, but if used uses only the records specified by the criteria in the calculation.

Table of Functions

@DSUM(*block,column,criteria*)   Sums the entries in a numeric field. The criteria portion of the argument is optional, but if used sums only the records specified by the criteria.

@DVAR(*block,column,criteria*)   Calculates the variance of a numeric field. The criteria portion of the argument is optional, but if used uses only the records specified by the criteria for the calculation.

Appendix B
Table of Features

Keys	Action	Description
F1	Help	Displays the help screens.
F2	Edit	Lets you edit a cell entry.
Shift-F2	Debug	Enters Macro Debug mode.
Alt-F2	Macro Menu	Displays the macro menu.
F3	Choices	Activates menu bar, zooms list, displays block names.
Shift-F3	Macros	Lists available macro commands.
Alt-F3	Functions	Lists the functions.
F4	Absolute Value	Makes cell addresses absolute.
F5	Goto	Moves selector to designated cell.
Shift-F5	Window Select	Lists open windows.
Alt-F5	Undo	Reverses previous action when Undo is enabled.
F6	Pane	Moves the selector to next open pane. When viewing a list of block names, displays block name notes.
Shift-F6	Next Window	Moves the selector to next open window.

Table of Features

Keys	Action	Description
Alt-F6	Zoom Window	Expands current window to full screen or shrinks window.
F7	Query	Executes previous query. In Graph Annotator, activates Proportional Resize mode.
Shift-F7	Select	Lets you extend the selection over a block of cells. In the File Manager, selects file in the file list.
Alt-F7	All Select	Selects or deselects all files in the File Manager.
F8	Table	Repeats the last what-if command.
Shift-F8	Move	In the File Manager, moves the selected files to the clipboard, so you can paste them in another drive or directory.
F9	Calc	Recalculates formulas in the spreadsheet.
Shift-F9	Copy	In the File Manager, copies the files selected in the active file list and stores them in the clipboard, so you can paste them in another drive or directory.
F10	Graph	Displays the current graph.
Shift-F10	Paste	In the File Manager, inserts copied or moved files into the specified directory.

145

Appendix C
DOS Primer

This section explains the basics of DOS and some of the procedures you'll use when working with it.

DOS is your computer's Disk Operating System. It functions as a go-between program that lets the various components of your computer system talk with one another. Whenever you type anything using your keyboard, move your mouse, or print a file, DOS interprets the commands and coordinates the task. The following sections explain how to run DOS on your computer, how to use DOS to manage your disks and directories, and how to make backup copies of the Quattro Pro program disks.

Starting DOS

To run Quattro Pro, you must have a hard disk. And if you have a hard disk, DOS is probably already installed on the hard disk. When you turn on your computer, DOS automatically loads. You will see a prompt on-screen that looks something like C:> or C>.

Working with Disks

The basic DOS commands deal with three elements: disks, directories on the disk, and files in the directories. In this section, you'll learn the basic DOS commands for working with disks.

Changing Disk Drives

Once DOS is loaded, you should see a *prompt* (also known as the DOS prompt) on-screen that looks something like A:> or A> (or C:> or B:>). This prompt tells you which disk drive is currently active. If you have a hard disk, the disk is usually labeled C. (Most computers have only one hard disk, but it may be treated as several disks: C, D, E, F, and so on.) The floppy disk drives, the drives located on the front of your computer, are drives A and B. If you have only one floppy drive, it's usually A and you have no drive B. If you have two floppy drives, the top or left drive is usually A, and the bottom or right drive is B. You can activate a different drive at any time by performing the following steps:

1. Make sure there's a formatted disk in the drive you want to activate. (Formatting is explained in the next section.)

2. Type the letter of the drive followed by a colon. For example, type `a:`. (You can type DOS commands in uppercase or lowercase characters.)

3. Press Enter. The DOS prompt changes to show that the drive you selected is now active.

147

Formatting Floppy Disks

Before you can store files on a floppy disk, you must *format* the disk.

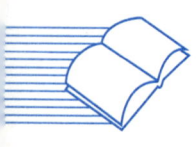

What Is Formatting? The formatting procedure creates a map on the disk that later tells DOS where to find the information you stored on it. Be careful when formatting because this procedure erases any existing information from the disk.

Disk Sizes and Densities The disk must be the same physical size as the drive you're using for formatting (5.25 inch or 3.5 inch). Disks also come in different densities, for example, double-density or high-density. The following instructions assume you are formatting a diskette that has the same maximum capacity as the drive (for example, a 360K or 720K diskette in a double-density drive or a 1.2M or 1.44M diskette in a high-density drive). Although you can format a double-density disk in a high-density drive, you will have to add a switch to the FORMAT command to do so. Refer to the DOS documentation.

1. Change to the drive and directory that contain your DOS files. For example, if your DOS files are in C:\DOS, type `cd\dos` at the C> prompt and press Enter. For information on changing directories, skip ahead to "Changing to a Directory."

2. Insert the blank floppy disk you want to format into floppy drive A or B.

3. Type `format a:` or `format b:` and press Enter. A message appears telling you to insert the disk (which you have already done).

4. Press Enter. DOS begins formatting the disk. When formatting is complete, DOS may display a message asking if you want to name the disk.

5. To name the disk, type a name (up to 11 characters) and press Enter. A message appears asking if you want to format another disk.

6. Type `y` if you want to format additional disks and then repeat all steps. Otherwise, type `N` to quit.

Labeling Disks If you know which files you're going to store on a formatted disk, you should label the disk with the names of the files and the current date. Write on the labels before sticking them to the disk; the pressure of a pen point can damage the fragile surface of a floppy disk. If you've already stuck the label to the disk, write on the label gently with a felt tip pen.

Using DISKCOPY To Make Backups of the Quattro Pro Program Disks

Before you install Quattro Pro on your hard disk, you should make *backup copies* of the original program disks. By using backups to install the program, you avoid the risk of damaging the original disks.

Appendix C

Obtain a set of blank disks that match the original program disks in number, size, and density. For example, if your copy of Quattro Pro came on three high-density 5.25-inch disks, obtain three blank high-density 5.25-inch disks. The type of disk should be marked on the package. Because the DISKCOPY command copies the entire disk, you don't have to format the blank disks before you begin.

Write-Protect the Original Disks To prevent the original program disks from getting damaged during the copying process, write-protect the disks. For 5.25-inch disks, stick a write-protect label over the notch on the side of the disk. For 3.5-inch disks, slide the write-protect tab so you can see through the window.

1. Change to the drive that contains the DOS program files. For example, type `c:` and press Enter.

2. If the DISKCOPY file is in a separate directory, change to that directory. For example, if the file is in the C:\DOS directory, type `cd\dos` at the C:> prompt and press Enter.

3. Type `diskcopy a: a:` or `diskcopy b: b:`, depending on which drive you're using to make the copies.

4. Press Enter. A message appears telling you to insert the source diskette into the floppy drive.

5. Insert the original Quattro Pro disk you want to copy into the specified drive and press Enter. DOS copies as much of the disk into RAM as RAM can hold. A message appears telling you to insert the target diskette into the floppy drive.

6. Insert one of the blank disks into the floppy drive and press Enter. DOS copies the information from RAM onto the blank disk. If DOS was able to copy the entire disk in one step, it displays a message asking if you want to copy another disk. If DOS could not copy the disk in one step, it displays a message telling you to insert the source disk.

7. Follow the on-screen prompts until DOS displays a message asking if you want to copy another disk.

8. Remove the disk from the drive and label it with the same name and number that appears on the original disk.

9. If you need to copy another original disk, press Y and go back to step 5. Continue until you copy all the original disks.

10. When you're done copying disks, type N when asked if you want to copy another disk.

11. Put the original disks back in their box and store them in a safe place.

Changing to a Directory

Before you can work with the files in a given directory, you need to change to that directory. The following steps tell you how:

1. Change to the drive that contains the directory. For example, type c: and press Enter.

Appendix C

2. Type `cd\`*`directory`*, where *directory* is the name of the directory you want to access. (For example, type `cd\qpro`.)

3. Press Enter.

The backslash (\) separates the names of the directories, giving DOS a *path* to follow to locate the directory at the end of the path. Use the backslash to separate all directories and subdirectories in a command line. A sample command line might look like this:

```
cd\forests\trees\maples
```

Is That All?

Now that you have Quattro Pro with its File Manager, you don't need to know much more about DOS. You can use the File Manager to perform most of the operations commonly performed using DOS, such as creating directories and copying and moving files. For more information on file management, refer to Lesson 21.

If you want more information about using DOS, you may want to read *The First Book of MS-DOS* by Jack Nimersheim, published by Sams.

Index

Symbols

#AND# (logical AND) operator, 43
#NOT# (logical NOT) operator, 43
#OR# (logical OR) operator, 43
' (left-align text), 26
" (right-align text), 26
^ (center text), 26
^ (exponentiation) operator, 32
* (multiplication) operator, 31-33
+ (addition) operator, 31-33
+/- value format, 74
- (subtraction) operator, 31-33
/ (active menu bar) keyboard shortcut, 7
/ (division) operator, 31-33
< (less than) operator, 43
<= (less than or equal to) operator, 43
< > (less than or greater than but not equal to) operator, 43
= (equal to) operator, 43
> (greater than) operator, 43
>= (greater than or equal to) operator, 43

A-B

Absolute Value feature, 144
Align option, 22
All Select feature, 144
Alt-F5 (undo change) keyboard shortcut, 65
Assign Names command, 122
Auto Width feature, 68
Black shading option, 82

C

Calc (calculate) option, 22
Calc (recalculate) feature, 145
cells
    addresses, 51
    blocks, 51
        destination, 63
        moving, 64-65
        selecting, 51-55
        source, 63
    changing, 65
    copying, 36-37, 63
    creating, 9
    deleting, 62
    editing, 60-61
    formatting, 63
    graphs, 104-105
    lines, 80-81
    locating, 58
    naming, 56-57, 59
    protecting, 79
    ranges, 39, 51, 53-55, 58
    references, 36-37
    shading, 81-83
    styles, 84-88
    text, 78

153

character modes, 4
Choices feature, 144
color, 112
Color command, 101
Column Width command, 67
columns, 9
   adding, 123
   deleting, 72
   inserting, 70-72
   width, 66-69
comma value format, 73
command button, 20
commands
   accessing, 21
   Assign Names, 122
   Color, 101
   Column Width, 67
   Copy, 22, 63
   Copy Special, 63
   Font Table, 77
   Guide, 101
   Help, 101
   Line Drawing, 80
   Move, 64
   Next, 101
   Numeric Format, 75, 85
   Previous, 101
   Quit, 101
   Rename, 138
   Reset Width, 67
   Ruler, 101
   Save As, 48
   Unzoom, 102
   Zoom, 102
context-sensitive, 5
control pane, 133-135
Copy command, 22, 63
Copy feature, 145
Copy Special command, 63
Create dialog box, 110
Create Names dialog box, 58
Ctrl-A (Alignment command) keyboard shortcut, 27, 78
Ctrl-E (delete cell contents) keyboard shortcut, 62
Ctrl-F (Numeric Format command) keyboard shortcut, 75
Ctrl-G (Fast Graph command) keyboard shortcut, 105
Ctrl-I (Insert Rows or Columns) keyboard shortcut, 72
Ctrl-M (move command) keyboard shortcut, 65
Ctrl-S (Save) shortcut key, 19
Ctrl-W (column width) keyboard shortcut, 67
Ctrl-X (exit quickly) speed key, 8
currency value format, 73
Customize Series option, 112

D

data
   entry option, 85
   formulas, 24
   labels, 24
   point, 104
   values, 24
Database menu, 125
database statistical functions, 142-143
databases
   components, 120-121
   creating, 122-123
   printing, 132
   records, 120-123, 127-131
   saving, 123
   sorting, 124-127
date value format, 74
date function, 141
dates, 30
Delete option, 22
destination blocks, 63
Destination option, 97

Index

dialog boxes, 7-8, 19-21
   command buttons, 46
   Create, 110
   Create Names, 58
   Graph Customize, 113
   Graph Overall, 115
   Open File, 49
   Print Layout Options, 89
   Save File, 46-47
   selecting, 20-21
directories, 136, 151-152
directory tree pane, 133, 136
disks
   backups, 149-151
   drives, 147
   floppy, 148-149
   labeling, 149
   write-protect, 150
DOS, 7, 146-147

E

Edit feature, 144
Edit menu, 58
EDIT mode, 22
Erase option, 22
exiting, 7-8
Extend mode, 53

F

F1 F3 (Help topics access)
   keyboard shortcut, 6
Fast Graph command, 105
features
   Absolute Value, 144
   All Select, 144
   Calc (recalculate), 145
   Choices, 144
   Copy, 145
   Edit, 144
   Functions, 144
   Goto, 144

   Graph, 145
   Help, 5-6, 144
   Macro Menu, 144
   Macros, 144
   Move, 145
   Next Window, 144
   Pane, 144
   Paste, 145
   Select, 144
   Sort, 124
   Table, 144
   Undo, 65, 144
   Zoom Window, 144
fields, 120
file list pane, 133-135
File Manager, 133-136
files
   closing, 48-49
   copying, 137
   erasing, 138
   locating, 47
   managing, 133-136
   moving, 137
   naming, 46, 138
   opening, 49-50
   retrieving, 49-50
   saving, 47
   selecting, 136-137
   viewing, 50
fill patterns, 112
financial function, 140-141
Fit option, 22
fixed value format, 73
Font option, 22, 85
Font Table command, 77
fonts, 75-77
footers, 89-91
formulas, 24-25
   entering, 31-35, 60
   settings, 37-38
functions
   arguments, 40
   assembling, 41

155

database statistical, 142-143
date, 141
elements, 40
entering, 39-40
financial, 140-141
list, 41
mathematical, 139-140
name, 40
statistical, 139
string, 140
time, 141
values, 39
Functions feature, 144

G

general value format, 73
Goto feature, 144
graph, 117-118
Graph Annotator, 116-119
Graph Customize dialog box, 113
Graph feature, 145
Graph Overall dialog box, 115
Graphics Printer, 97
graphs
  annotating, 116-119
  cells, 104-105
  color, 112
  creating, 103-109
  enhancing, 112-116
  fill patterns, 112
  formatting, 115-116
  inserting, 111
  legends, 107-109
  printing, 119
  retrieving, 110
  saving, 110
  titles, 107-109
  types, 103-104
  viewing, 106-107
Grey shading option, 82
Guide command, 101

H-I

hard copies, 102
headers, 89-91
Help command, 101
Help feature, 5-6, 144
highlights, 55
input lines, 11
Insert option, 22

K

keyboard shortcuts
  / (active menu bar), 7
  Alt-F5 (undo change), 65
  Ctrl-X (exit quickly), 8
  Ctrl-A (Alignment command), 27, 78
  Ctrl-E (delete cell contents), 62
  Ctrl-F (Numeric Format command), 75
  Ctrl-G (Fast Graph command), 105
  Ctrl-I (Insert Rows or Columns), 72
  Ctrl-M (move command), 65
  Ctrl-S (Save), 19
  Ctrl-W (column width), 67
  F1 F3 (Help topics access), 6
  Shift-F8 (move files), 137
  Shift-F9 (copy file), 137
  Shift-Tab (move back one option), 21
keyboards, selecting, 18, 21

L

Label Order option, 127
labels
  aligning, 26-27
  default settings, 27
  entering, 24-28, 60

Index

Line Drawing command, 80
line drawing option, 85
lines, 80-81
logical operators, 43

M

Macro Menu feature, 144
Macros feature, 144
mathematical functions, 139-140
memory, random-access, 45
menu bars, 11
menus
  Database, 125
  Edit, 58
  Print, 89, 98
  pull-down, 3, 16
  Style, 67
  switching, 19
modes
  changing, 4
  character, 4
  EDIT, 22
  Extend, 53
  indicator, 11, 53-55
  overstrike, 62
  POINT, 53-55
  Print Preview, 99-102
  READY, 22
  screen, 2-3
mouse
  clicking, 14
  dialog boxes, 20
  dragging, 14
    columns, 67
    rows, 70
  left-handed, 15
  options, 17-18
  pointing, 11, 14
  selecting, 52, 55
Move command, 64
Move feature, 145
Move option, 22

N

Name option, 22
Next command, 101
Next Window feature, 144
None shading option, 82
Numbers Before Labels option, 127
Numeric Format command, 75, 85

O

objects, 118-119
Open File dialog box, 49
operators
  logical, 43-44
    #AND# (logical AND), 43
    #NOT# (logical NOT), 43
    #OR# (logical OR), 43
    < (less than), 43
    <= (less than or equal to), 43
    <> (less than or greater than but not equal to), 43
    = (equal to), 43
    > (greater than), 43
    >= (greater than or equal to), 43
  mathematical
    ^ (exponentiation), 32
    * (multiplication), 31-33
    + (addition), 31-33
    - (subtraction), 31-33
    / (division), 31-33
    combinations, 32
    order, 33
option button, 20
options
  Alignment, 22, 85
  Calc (calculate), 22
  Copy, 22
  Customize Series, 112
  Data Entry, 85

157

Delete, 22, 72
Destination, 97
Erase, 22
Fit, 22
Font, 22, 85
Insert, 22
Label Order, 127
Line Drawing, 85
Move, 22
Name, 22
Numbers Before Labels, 127
Numeric Format, 75, 85
Overall, 112-116
printing, 97-98
Query, 131
selecting, 17-18
shading, 82, 85
Sort Rows/Columns, 127
Style, 22
Sum, 22
X-Axis, 112-115
Y-Axis, 113-115
Overall option, 112, 115-116
overstrike mode, 62

P

pages
   breaking, 94
   defaults, 94
   length, 89, 92
   margins, 89, 92-94
   printing, 89
Pane feature, 144
Paste feature, 145
paths, 47
percent value format, 74
POINT mode, 53-55
Previous command, 101
Print Layout Options dialog
   box, 89
Print menu, 89, 98
Print Preview mode, 99-102

printers
   Graphics, 97
   selecting, 96-97
printing, 89
   databases, 132
   destinations, 97
   footers, 89
   graphs, 119
   hard copies, 102
   headers, 89
   options, 97-98
   previewing, 99-102
   scaling, 95
   settings, 95
   worksheets, 102
prompt, 147
pull-down menu, 3, 16

Q

Query option, 131, 144
Quit command, 101

R

random access memory (RAM), 45
ranges, 39, 51, 53-55, 58
READY mode, 22
recalculation settings, 37-38
records
   adding, 120-123
   defining, 127-128
   extracting, 131
   locating, 127-131
Rename command, 138
Reset Width command, 67
rows, 9
   deleting, 72
   height, 69-70
   inserting, 70-72
Ruler command, 101

S

Save As command, 48
Save File dialog box, 46-47
scaling, 95
scientific value format, 73
screen modes, 2-3, 19
scrolling, 15
search criteria table, 128-129
Select feature, 144
selector, 11-14
shading option, 85
Shift-F8 (move files) keyboard
 shortcut, 137
Shift-F9 (copy file) keyboard
 shortcut, 137
Shift-Tab (move back one option)
 keyboard command, 21
Sort feature, 124
Sort Rows/Columns option, 127
source blocks, 63
speed key combinations, *see*
 keyboard shortcuts
SpeedBar, 21-22
starting, 1-2
statistical functions, 139
status lines, 11
string functions, 140
Style menu, 67
Style option, 22
styles, , 84-88
Sum option, 22

T

Table feature, 144
text, 19, 26, 78
time functions, 141
TurboSum, 41-43

U-V

Undo feature, 65, 144
Unzoom command, 102
values, 24
 dates, 25
 entering, 28-29, 60
 formatting, 29, 73-75
  +/-, 74
  comma, 73
  currency, 73
  date, 74
  fixed, 73
  general, 73
  percent, 74
  scientific, 73
 numeric entries, 25
 ranges, 39

W

windows, 50
worksheets
 closing, 48-49
 creating, 24-26
 graphs, 111
 naming, 46
 opening, 49-50
 printing, 102
 retrieving, 49-50
 saving, 45-48
 screens, 10
 switching, 50
WYSIWYG (What You See Is
 What You Get), 2-4

X-Z

X-Axis option, 112-115
Y-Axis option, 112-115
Zoom command, 102
Zoom Window feature, 144

159